The Fully Devoted Life Prayer Journal

John Gregory

drink
p u b l i s h i n g
2866 56th Avenue Circle East
Bradenton, Florida 34203
drinkpublishing.com

The Fully Devoted Life Prayer Journal: A 65-day Journey Through Your
Testimony, Time, Talents, and Treasures

By John Gregory

Published by Drink Publishing
9607 State Road 70 East
Bradenton, Florida 34202
www.outcomepublishing.com

First Edition

Printed in the United States of America

1. Religion: Spirituality General
2. Self-Help: Spiritual
3. Religion: Christian Life – Personal Growth

TABLE OF CONTENTS

Introduction

Not all journeys just sort of happen, but the creation of this volume did. After months of preparation and seeking God's direction, our pastor at Woodland the Community Church, Tim Passmore, led the congregation through a 9-week spiritual transformation called *Imagine...the fully devoted life*. He asked the congregation to commit to attend nine weeks of weekend worship services and to also join a small group to study together four topics – testimony, time, talents, and treasure.

As part of the prayer initiative for this 9-week journey, I committed to writing daily emails that were forwarded to each person connected to a small group. Following the theme of the number 9, each email ended with a prayer suggestion for praying at 9am or 9pm. Having done this assignment previously for another campaign, it seemed pretty straightforward. However, the approach this time became quite different. Before, the emails were pretty much a bullet list of things to lift up in prayer each day. For some reason as these nine weeks went on, these emails took on more of a devotional nature coinciding with the weekly material in the small group study guide. The desire for deeper communicating and meditating rather than petitioning praying became the target.

Toward the end of the congregation's journey, the idea of putting these emails into a book was presented. That's why I say this volume just sort of happened. On the flip side of that thought though, does anything with God just sort of happen? I'm inclined to think not. It is my prayer that, whether you are using this prayer journal along with your study through *Imagine* or whether you are just seeking some furthering of your daily conversations with God, at the end of your 65 days you will say, "That was a great trip."

Journey On,

John

assessment

Good Morning – Day 1,

s we start this journey together, particularly through this first week, we are focusing in several ways to assess our spiritual lives. One of my favorite chapters, Psalm 139, is David's way of asking God to assess him. He spends the majority of the chapter showing how who God is just blows his mind. Because of God's incredible nature, David ends the chapter with this prayer:

"Search me, God, and know my heart; test me and know my anxious thoughts. See if there is any offensive way in me, and lead me in the way everlasting." (vs. 23-24, TNIV)

I encourage you to pause at 9am or 9pm today and allow your understanding of God to move you to echo David's prayer.

assessment

Good Morning - Day 2,

A s we continue this week of assessment, one question we can ask ourselves is how thankful we are to God for all he has done for us. In our assessing questions for the testimony section, we evaluate our thanking God in how we share our faith with others. In Psalm 57, David declares,

"I will thank you, Lord, among all the people. I will sing your praises among the nations.
For your unfailing love is as high as the heavens. Your faithfulness reaches to the clouds." (vs. 9-10, NLT)

In your prayer time today at 9am or 9pm, thank God along with David and repeat his final thought of that psalm,

"Be exalted, O God, above the highest heavens. May your glory shine over all the earth." (vs. 11, NLT)

assessment

Good Morning - Day 3,

I was reading in Luke 20 this morning and came across the passage where the chief priests tried to trick Jesus by asking him was it lawful to give tribute to Caesar or not. Here's how Luke describes Jesus' response:

"But he perceived their craftiness, and said to them, 'Show me a denarius. Whose likeness and inscription does it have?' They said, 'Caesar's.' He said to them, 'Then render to Caesar the things that are Caesar's and to God the things that are God's.' And they were not able in the presence of the people to catch him in what he said, but marveling at his answer they became silent." *(vs. 23-26, ESV)*

Knowing the denarius bore Caesar's image thus making it his, the question we should ask ourselves is what has God's image, what should we give to him in tribute. According to Genesis, we, his creation, bear his image. So the answer to what should we give to God is ourselves. Here's how Paul put it: *"Therefore, I urge you, brothers and sisters, in view of God's mercy, to offer your bodies as a living sacrifice, holy and pleasing to God--this is true worship." (Romans 12:1, TNIV)*

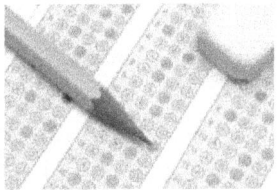

In your prayer time today at 9am or 9pm, thank God for creating you in his image and ask him to help you bear it well.

assessment

11

Good Morning - Day 4,

O ccasionally I wake up with songs in my head. Today was one of those days - two songs actually. The first song was the first verse and chorus of a children's chorus that says,
"Jesus loves me this I know, for the Bible tells me so.
Children all to him belong; they are weak, but he is strong.
Yes, Jesus loves me.
Yes, Jesus loves me.
Yes, Jesus loves me.
The Bible tells me so."[1]

The second song following behind that was the chorus to a hymn which says,
"This is my story, this is my song.
Praising my Savior all the day long.
This is my story, this is my song.
Praising my Savior all the day long."[2]

The singing I hear in my head is usually reminiscent of being in church and hearing the congregation lift their voices up in unity declaring the love of God. We're not in church together today to declare it, but we sure can declare it to others who need to hear it, maybe just to be reminded or maybe to hear it for the first time.

In your prayer time today at 9am or 9pm, thank God for loving you and ask him to show you someone who needs to hear today that God loves them.

assessment

Good Morning - Day 5,

L ooking over some old entries in my journal today, I came across some notes based on a verse that could definitely help us pursue the fully devoted life. It is found in Proverbs 21:21 and it promises

"Whoever pursues righteousness and unfailing love will find life, righteousness, and honor." (NLT)

Here are some bullet thoughts from this short verse:
- Real life is found in righteousness and love.
- Honor and life are found only when pursued.
- Pursuing is an action verb. Righteousness and love require action. They are not automatic components of living.

In your prayer time today at 9am or 9pm, declare to God your desire for life and honor; commit to pursue righteousness and love.

assessment

Good Morning - Day 6,

R ecently, while reading a book by a pastor in Texas, I came across a different teaching then I had heard before on the word *repent*. Working through our assessing exercises probably results in our needing to repent of some things. To encourage you in that discipline, here are three paragraphs for you to consider:

> "The word repent is not a word designed in heaven to make you feel bad about who you are or what you've done. The word repent has a very significant meaning. *Re* means "to return." *Re-pent* means "to go back to a place." *Pent* is a word meaning "the highest position," such as a penthouse or pinnacle. So the word *repent* means "to go back to the place of highest position."

> What was the place of highest position for man? It was his status in the Garden of Eden where God and man walked and talked together in the cool of the evening as friends. That was before sin destroyed the relationship, and God and man were separated. Repentance is not designed to make you feel bad about yourself. God offers repentance so you can return to the Garden of Eden and walk and talk with Him as a personal friend.

> Repentance is not to shame you, embarrass you, or make you feel inferior or inadequate. Repentance is designed to get you into the presence of God. There is no other road. Repentance is the passport to renewing your relationship with God!"[3]

Doesn't that thought encourage to you pursue daily repentance? It does me. In your prayer time today at 9am or 9pm, ask the Holy Spirit to reveal your needs for repentance, and then thank him for allowing you to renew your relationship with him.

assessment

Good Morning - Day 7,

S tatement #4 in our assessment of our opening chapter asked us to evaluate this aspect regarding our time: *I daily practice the discipline of Bible study.*

When I think of this discipline, the verse that comes to my mind is 2 Timothy 2:15. Here's how that verse reads in the New Living Translation:

"Work hard so you can present yourself to God and receive His approval. Be a good worker, one who does not need to be ashamed and who correctly explains the word of truth." (NLT)

Here's a study note for this verse from the Discover God Study Bible:

> "Paul was a tentmaker by trade and often supported himself by this work. As he worked with the rough camel-hair cloth that was typically used for making a proper tent, he was careful to make the most of the pieces he had to work with, making straight cuts so sections could be easily and properly joined. That may be where he gets the imagery used here. The expression 'correctly explains the word of truth' is literally translated 'cuts it straight.' The best tents are made with straight cuts; the best living is made when the Bible is read honestly and 'cut straight.'"

In your prayer time today at 9am or 9pm, seek God's direction as you read his word to read it honestly. Ask him to cut it straight for you so you can then live today following that clear path.

assessment

testimony

Good Morning - Day 8,

J ust so you know, I don't normally share my dreams with masses of people, but here goes.

I woke up this morning around 3am from a dream unlike any other I've ever had leaving me with a feeling unlike any other I've ever had. In my dream, I was on a mission trip with a team from our church. We were ministering to young people in a foreign setting. We were gathered in a pretty good size room; it seemed like we had just finished some type of meeting, so people were just standing around talking. An awkward silence came over the room as we all focused on one of our female team members being verbally abused by a high-school-aged national boy. I interrupted him to intervene on the lady's behalf. The words I spoke to him seemed to land on the most hardened heart I have ever witnessed. As the people began dispersing from the awkward setting, the presence of cold reception to the truth felt tangible. It was as if you could feel the resistance from good and the choosing for evil. That's when I woke up.

Now what to make of the dream is your guess as good as mine. All I know is as I thought about the scene before I fell back to sleep, a verse came to my mind from Luke 19 that says, *"For the Son of Man came to seek and to save what was lost."* (verse 10, TNIV)

My routine for reading my Bible is while I am eating my bowl of cereal each morning. Wouldn't you know it, just a few hours from dreaming that scene, the *Imagine* quiet time I read was from Luke 19. Coincidence? Highly unlikely.

In your prayer time today at 9am or 9pm, thank Jesus for coming to seek you when you were lost. Ask the Holy Spirit to grow in your heart a like passion to seek and to save those who are lost.

testimony

Good Morning - Day 9,

I'm still reading in Luke for my personal quiet time. Today I read verses 39-46 of chapter 22; it's the scene of Jesus' prayer in the Garden of Gethsemane before he is arrested. There is an interesting phrase in verse 39 that caught my attention. The phrase is "as was his custom." This verse does nothing more than setting up the scene of the story. It is just describing where Jesus was going, who was with him. I don't think Luke had to put that phrase in there. I believe he did, though, for a reason.

Now, I'm not Luke, but I have a hunch what his point is with this phrase. I believe his point is simply that Jesus was doing something or going somewhere that he had done or been several times. In other words, this was routine. Why is that a big deal, or is it?

Well, to me, at the point of my reading, it was - for 2 reasons:

1)If we are going to practice the discipline of prayer that Jesus did in this scene, it takes having a solid routine. A prayer life can't grow if it isn't nurtured. I need to have a routine to my prayer life.

2)Part of a solid routine is having a secure location for the routine. Apparently this place was such a place for Jesus. I mentioned yesterday my routine for my Bible reading. I sit in the same chair at my dining table. That is my routine place.

In your prayer time today at 9am or 9pm, thank God for meeting with you; commit to furthering your relationship with him by reserving the right place at the right time that allows you to best grow together.

testimony

Good Morning - Day 10,

L ast week one of our Imagine quiet times took us to Acts 4. In verse 20 Peter and John say, *"As for us, we cannot help speaking about what we have seen and heard."* (TNIV) This was their final reply to being questioned about their work in the name of Jesus. I'd like to share a little of what I have seen and heard just over the last few days.

Friday - I had been asked by a couple to come visit their new business and pray with them as they prepare to open their doors. What I saw on Friday was evidence of a lot of hard work, clear vision, and dedication to provide the best service possible to their clients. What I heard was testimony convincing me that this couple has a God-given call, and they are committed to fulfilling it out of their love for their Savior, which has given them a true love for those walking through their business door.

Saturday - I run. Along with a few friends, I ran a 10k at Myakka State Park benefiting a local organization for families with children who have disabilities. What did I see that morning? I saw a church member and her daughter using their gifts and talents to organize and serve an event birthed from their own experiences of living with disabled children. I saw another church couple, who not realizing it, illustrated their acceptance of others by taking the time to talk with my friends, who are not Christians, and just share life with them after having just met them.

That afternoon before coming to church, I stopped by Sarasota Memorial Hospital to visit with a man who had undergone surgery on Thursday. The surgery was to remove a lung which had been treated with chemo for a cancerous tumor. What did I

testimony

hear that afternoon? I heard a man proclaim how prayers have resulted in the lab worker calling and asking where the tumor was supposed to be in the lung because they could not find evidence of it. He spoke of how his bout with lung cancer has impacted five friends and family members to stop smoking. He spoke how prayers from people spread over six states have resulted in evidence that God continues to hear and answer prayer. I also heard from his mother who shared how grateful she was for God's healing in her son's body.

Before praying today at 9am or 9pm, take time to pause and remember what you have seen and heard from the work of God and his people over the last few days. In your prayer, thank God for showing himself to you and commit to share with others what you have seen and heard.

testimony

Good Morning - Day 11,

I am wrapping up reading through Luke. This morning I finished reading chapter 23, which recounts the crucifixion of Jesus. Talk about some people who "saw and heard," look at how Luke paints the reactions of those who witnessed this event.

verse 47: *"Now when the centurion saw what had taken place, he praised God, saying, 'Certainly this man was innocent!'"*

Matthew and Mark recount that he declared that Jesus must have been the Son of God.

verse 48: *"And all the crowds that had assembled for this spectacle, when they saw what had taken place, returned home beating their breasts."*

Their reaction was one of grief and repentance.

verses 50-53: *"Now there was a man named Joseph, from the Jewish town of Arimathea. He was a member of the council, a good and righteous man, who had not consented to their decision and action; and he was looking for the kingdom of God. This man went to Pilate and asked for the body of Jesus. Then he took it down and wrapped it in a linen shroud and laid him in a tomb cut in stone, where no one had ever yet been laid."* (ESV)

testimony

Joseph, described by Matthew as a disciple of Jesus, went beyond just seeing and hearing. His actions - going to Pilate and then

burying Jesus in his own tomb, an example of investing recorded in all four Gospels - reveal his strong devotion to all he had seen and heard. I like Luke's description of Joseph as "looking for the kingdom."

Think about this. The account of the first church recorded for us in Acts, also written by Luke, is remarkable. Who do you think made up the core of that remarkable church? Uh huh - these people right here. They were fully devoted to what they had seen and heard

allowing them not only to impact their community but to lay the foundation for the history of the church as we know it. Oh, the power of the cross.

As you pray today at 9am or 9pm, thank the Holy Spirit for his written account of the cross, thank Jesus for his sacrifice, and thank God for those he used to establish his church. Ask God to allow the scene of the cross to be impressed in your heart causing you to be an agent of impact for him.

testimony

Good Morning - Day 12,

T he other day I drove by a church that had this saying on its sign: "The Big Bang Theory? Sure. God spoke and Bang!"

This week the tag line for our focus is imagine a life that remembers where it started. Thinking about that this morning, my mind went to the Genesis account of creation. Anne Graham Lotz published a book, *God's Story: Finding Meaning for Your Life in Genesis,* about 10 years ago in which she helps you remember how we all got started by looking at the first eleven chapters of Genesis. Check out this story she shared about Isaac Newton:

> "Sir Isaac Newton once had a miniature model of the solar system in his office. The sun was positioned in the center of the model with the various planets displayed in orbit around it. One day a fellow scientist walked into his study and when he saw it exclaimed, 'My! What an exquisite thing this is! Who made it?' Sir Isaace Newton replied, 'Nobody.'
>
> The scientist looked amazed as he said skeptically, 'You must think I am a fool. Of course somebody made it, and he is a genuis.'
> Sir Isaace Newton got up, walked around his desk, and put his hand on the shoulder of his friend as he said earnestly, 'This thing is but a puny imitation of a much grander system whose laws you and I know. I am not able to convince you that this mere toy is without a

testimony

designer and maker; yet you profess to believe that the great original from which the design is taken has come into being without either designer or maker. Now tell me, by what sort of reasoning do you reach such incongruous conclusions?'"[5]

At times we are all in need of remembering that God is our creator. Before you pray today at 9am or 9pm, take a look around you. Wherever you are, you can see evidence of God by his fingerprint on creation. Thank God for the truth, for finding meaning for your life through it, and implore him to continue shedding the light of truth into our darkened world.

testimony

Good Morning - Day 13,

Each year our nation takes notice of what the date 9/11 now means to us. One question/statement you hear from people is the retelling of where they were on that morning in 2001 when they first heard the news. "Where were you...what were you doing...well, I remember I had just walked into the office when..." It is now a part of our life story.

Thinking on that last night as I drove home from Small Group, I thought how cool it will be when we get to hear from some other fully devoted followers in heaven tell one of their life changing stories. Like the guy, trying to reassure his family that Pharoah's army would never get close enough to hurt them, who saw out of the corner of his eye the waters of the Red Sea begin to create a pathway to safety. Or the older brother of David whose jaw dropped as he watched his little brother take out his silly sling shot and proceed to show Goliath what faith in the God of Israel could do. Or the look on Elijah's face while he recounts how he had never ran faster in his life as the day when he ran back to Jezreel after calling down fire from heaven and having the prophets of Baal slain.

The words of a traditional spiritual asks four similar questions of those who were there the day all our life stories changed:

testimony

"Were you there when they crucified my Lord?"
"Were you there when they nailed Him to the tree?"
"Were you there when they laid Him in the tomb?"
"Were you there when He rose up from the dead?"

The exclamatory replies to these questions are,

"O! Sometimes it causes me to tremble, tremble, tremble!"
and *"O! Sometimes I feel like shouting glory, glory, glory!"*[6]

As you pray today at 9am or 9pm, recount with God a moment in your life that you remember he was there. Thank God for his faithfulness, mercy, and power. Ask him for an opportunity to tell that story to somebody in need of their own moment with God.

testimony

Good Morning - Day 14,

Here's a question for you: Who comes to mind in the Bible as a person who had a great story to tell about their life before meeting Christ and how their life changed after meeting him? Lots of options may come to your mind, but I'd like to take your mind to one particular guy. Mark 5 and Luke 8 tell us about a man who definitely had a story to tell about the change in his life because of meeting Jesus.

This is the story of the demon-possessed man that lived in the tombs. He went by the name of Legion, which the demons exclaimed stood for "we are many." We know that a full Roman legion typically had more than 6,000 men. We don't know if this guy was under the influence of that many demons, but it's clear that he was filled with a whole bunch of them. I can't imagine what that must have been like. Can you imagine being one of those "pig tenders" who watched this encounter between Jesus and this scary guy ending with your 2,000 pigs being overtaken by the same crazy actions as this man causing them to run down the lake bank and drown? My reaction would have probably been something like, "No wonder he was so crazy! I'm glad those pigs were here, or that could have been me."

The ending of the story is pretty telling too, right? Mark tells with his last seven verses how no one could keep their mouth shut about what they witnessed. The great thing to note about this man returning home is his spreading the

testimony

news of how Jesus had released him from his bondage. And check this out - the Decapolis where he returned to share his story was a league of ten originally free Greek cities. What's the big deal? These people weren't Jews. It is possible that Mark was indicating to us that this story resulted in the gospel spreading to these Gentiles for the first time. Crazy as it may sound, you may be a Christian today because of the testimony of this demon-possessed man. Thank God for the pigs, eh?

As you pray today at 9am or 9pm, thank Jesus for ministering to all people. Ask him to fill you up with such gratitude for your bondage release that you just can't keep your mouth shut.

testimony

Good Morning - Day 15,

When we are challenged about sharing our story, it seems the number one reason given for not sharing it as we should has to do with some sort of fear. As a form of encouragement, here are some examples of Biblical characters that faced their fears.

Esther (Esther 4)
She knew of a plot to kill her people. Yet, she was in a weird spot. If she spoke up to the king without being asked about it, she could be killed herself. With the encouragement of her cousin Mordecai, she knew she was in her position by no accident. After fasting for three days, she faced the fear saying, "If I perish, I perish."

Shadrach, Meshach and Abednego (Daniel 3)
These guys also stood up to a king. When threatened with fire and a challenge to their god, they replied, *"We do not need to defend ourselves before you in this matter. If we are thrown into the blazing furnace, the God we serve is able to save us from it, and he will rescue us from your hand."* Nebuchadnezzar's own words sum up how the story ended: *"No other god can save in this way."* (verses 16-17, 29)

Stephen (Acts 7)
He stood before one of the groups responsible for having Jesus killed. Talk about a reason to fear. Well, he passed the test with flying colors. So much that as he felt the wrath of man he *"looked up to heaven and saw the glory of*

testimony

God, and Jesus standing at the right hand of God...and prayed, 'Lord Jesus, receive my spirit...do not hold this sin against them.'" (verses 55, 59-60)

As you pray today at 9am or 9pm, confess your fears. Thank the Holy Spirit for the faith modeled by believers throughout church history. Ask him to fill you with that same faith in order to defeat your fears bringing victory in your life and those with whom you share your story.

testimony

Good Morning - Day 16,

As we share our story we may struggle with the timetable of people's reception of the truth. I'd like to share an example of a true story, told by Gary Poole from Willow Creek Church in Chicago, of how prayer coupled with sharing your story go hand in hand.

Shortly after Rita Cuffey became a follower of Christ, she began praying for her husband Jim. An exceptionally brilliant, intelligent man at 40 years of age, Jim held a doctorate from Harvard and was a professor of astronomy at Indiana University - and he was a self-proclaimed atheist. "The more I learn, the more I'm convinced there is no God," he insisted.

In spite of his wife's conversion, Jim had no interest in Christianity, aside from occasionally criticizing and poking fun at it. Well-meaning friends from the Presbyterian church where Rita (and sometimes Jim) attended consistently shared their faith with Jim, approaching him with kindness and gentleness. The pastor firmly, but lovingly, challenged Jim several times with the truth that he was a sinner in need of a Savior. "The real truth is your religion puts me off," Jim taunted. But it was also true that he was stubborn.

All throughout his forties, Jim refused to believe. But Rita didn't stop praying. "This is what God would want me to do," she'd often say. "It's consistent with Scripture that I pray for him." As Jim approached 50, Rita clung to verses like 2 Peter 3:9 ("The Lord isn't really being slow about his promise, as some people think. No, he is being patient for your sake. He does not want anyone to be destroyed, but

testimony

33

wants everyone to repent.") as she kept right on praying for him. When he turned 60, she still believed God wanted him to come to Christ. Rita prayed. She prayed even when everyone around her, including her children, kept telling her it probably wouldn't ever happen.

Even as Jim reached his seventies, Rita continued to plead with God on a daily basis that He would somehow get through to her husband. Rita would not, could not, let go of the hope that the Holy Spirit would soften this man's hardened heart. Right on through Jim's seventies and into his eighties, Rita prayed.

Finally it happened. Much to the astonishment of all his friends and family members, Jim came to the point where he humbled himself and put his faith and trust in Jesus Christ alone for forgiveness. It was a miracle. He was 85 years old. For 45 years Rita prayed. You can only imagine the tears of joy Rita shed on that momentous occasion.

Jim passed away two years later, and Rita grieved her loss with a deep sense of gratitude as she rested in the promises of Scripture that her husband was safe and secure, present with the one in whom he finally trusted. Her prayers were answered![7]

As you pray today at 9am or 9pm, declare your faith that God will honor your prayers for those who hear your story. Commit to never give up on the power of prayer.

testimony

Good Morning - Day 17,

T he first occupation of a witness discussed in this week's chapter is the doctor. Our doctor task is to see those around us with needs and to meet those needs. Not too hard to see people with needs these days, right? And the type of need - physical, financial, emotional, spiritual - is just as diverse as the people we see.

As I read this, the first Bible story that came to my mind was about the four guys who took their paralyzed friend to Jesus to be healed. These guys were determined to have their friend's need met. Mark 2:4 tells us just how determined they were: *"Since they could not get him to Jesus because of the crowd, they made an opening in the roof above Jesus by digging through it and then lowered the mat the man was lying on."* Because of their faith, Jesus not only healed their friend but also declared his sins forgiven. The impact of these guys' desire to have their friend's need met is given in verse 12: *"This amazed everyone and they praised God saying, 'We have never seen anything like this!'"* (TNIV)

As you pray today at 9am or 9pm, thank God for meeting your needs. Ask him to open your eyes today to someone's need. Determine to be prepared to get up on the roof.

testimony

Good Morning - Day 18,

Yesterday I wrote about the doctor occupation of a witness discussed in this week's chapter pointing out a Biblical illustration. I thought today I'd share with you some recent illustrations of Woodland doctors as a result of members going through Imagine.

Last Thursday I received the following prayer request from another Woodland doctor:
I am going through a very difficult time right now with my mother. Until today I have not spoken to her for 10 years. I've been praying that God fix this problem in my heart (and hers). I woke up this morning with an urge to speak to her. My mother does not have an ounce of God in her heart and desperately needs Him. Please help me pray that God can reach her and soften her heart. I told her today that I was concerned for her. I said she needs family and she needs people to love her and asked that she just let us back in. Please help me pray for her and my little brother and sisters.

Friday, a fellow Woodland doctor friend told me this story: His mother called him talking like he'd never heard her talk before. She had been fired from her job. She was so depressed about life that she was talking suicidal. Her need was obvious. He said the Holy Spirit made it clear to him what to do. He grabbed a copy of Rick Warren's book *The Purpose Driven Life* and drove to her house. He shared how she was loved and gave her the book. She just stared at it looking at the subtitle, "What on earth am I here for?"

testimony

She said, "That is exactly how I feel." He told me that she is reading the book and is talking with him like a changed person. His prayer is to see her let Christ meet her spiritual need.

Saturday I received this email about a Woodland doctor looking out for her daughter:

Fear is the main reason why my husband and I have a hard time sharing our story with others. We are afraid that someone will ask us something that we can't answer. Since we started this lesson, I can tell you that we both have shared our story with more than one person. One of those people just happens to be our eight-year-old daughter! How great is that? We will continue our journey through this lesson, and even after it is over, we will continue on this same path.

As you pray today at 9am or 9pm, praise God for the opportunity to doctor. Ask him to work through you and these three doctors to continue to meet needs.

testimony

Good Morning - Day 19,

T he third occupation of a witness discussed in this week's chapter is the marketing supervisor - being appointed by God to be a witness to a particular target. I can think of no better illustration of this than the Old Testament character of Jonah.

We can learn a lot from his story - like how not to answer God's call, which direction not to run in, or how to pray while waiting for a fish to recognize humans are normal diet food. But the truth I'd like to challenge you with from Jonah's story is that we don't have the right to reject the target God gives us. Let's be honest - some people on your target you'd prefer they'd be on someone else's. That neighbor, that coworker, that family member, or that home owner association board member. We all have one or more if we really get serious about it. These may be the very people that cause our fear or plain out obstinance to share our story. Obstinance, and I think it's fair to say probably prejudice, was Jonah's main issue with his God-given target of the people of Nineveh. That's why, when Jonah complained to God about his decision to spare his target, God replied, *"Is it right for you to be angry about this?"* (4:4, NLT)

Is it possible that you wish someone wasn't on your God-given target? As you pray today at 9am or 9pm, confess that to God. Ask him to come and fill your heart with love and to grow a desire to share that love with everyone on your target.

testimony

Good Morning - Day 20,

esterday we saw Jonah's not-so-good illustration of the witnessing occupation of the marketing supervisor. Today I'd like to share a good illustration of this occupation as well as the fourth occupation discussed in this week's chapter, the optometrist. Just to refresh your mind, the optometrist's task is to help correct bad spiritual vision. A character, again from the Old Testament, that illustrates both of these occupations well is Joseph.

Joseph's target included the following:

- Brothers who had thoughts of killing him but ended up easing their conscience by selling him into slavery
- His boss's wife who wrongly accused him of attempted rape
- Two fellow prison inmates, former employees of Pharaoh

Compare that with yours and how do you feel now? Well, Joseph apparently didn't mind his target because he viewed his life from the perspective that God was in charge. In Genesis 39, not once, not twice, not thrice, but four times the writer states that *"the Lord was with Joseph."* And his story clearly illustrates it. And he thought enough about God's work in his life to declare it by what he named his 2 boys; their names meant *"God has made me forget all my trouble"* and *"God has made me fruitful."* (Genesis 41) These names simply told his story to his target.

testimony

As for his illustration of optometry, he gives us one of the clearest examples of forgiveness in the Bible, helping his brothers with their spiritual vision. Understandably so, after their father died they feared that Joseph might reveal a hidden grudge against them

and *"pay us back for all the wrong we did to him."* (Genesis 50:15) He corrected their vision of the providence of God by replying, *"You intended to harm me, but God intended it all for good. He brought me to this position so I could save the lives of many people. No, don't be afraid. I will continue to take care of you and your children."* (50:20-21, NLT)

As you pray today at 9am or 9pm, ask God for ways to declare him to those on your target. Ask him for wisdom to share who he is to those with poor spiritual vision.

testimony

Good Morning - Day 21,

The subject I'd like to focus on today is forgiveness. Easy to say. Not so easy to do. As I read through the description of the spiritual surgical procedure of confession (*Imagine*, 55), my mind asked the question, "How often do Christians model this type of forgiveness to those with spiritual bad vision?" The first story that came to my mind happened two years ago. Here's a recap from the PA Dutch Country Welcome Center.

Following the tragic shooting of 10 Amish girls in a one-room Amish school in October 2006, reporters from throughout the world invaded Lancaster County, PA to cover the story. However, in the hours and days following the shooting a different, an unexpected story developed. In the midst of their grief over this shocking loss, the Amish community didn't cast blame, they didn't point fingers, they didn't hold a press conference with attorneys at their sides. Instead, they reached out with grace and compassion toward the killer's family. The afternoon of the shooting an Amish grandfather of one of the girls who was killed expressed forgiveness toward the killer, Charles Roberts. That same day Amish neighbors visited the Roberts family to comfort them in their sorrow and pain. Later that week the Roberts family was invited to the funeral of one of the Amish girls who had been killed. And Amish mourners outnumbered the non-Amish at Charles Roberts'

testimony

funeral. It's ironic that the killer was tormented for nine years by the pre-mature death of his young daughter. He never forgave God for her death. Yet, after he cold-bloodedly shot 10 innocent Amish school girls, the Amish almost immediately forgave him and showed compassion toward his family. In a world at war and in a society that often points fingers and blames others, this reaction was unheard of. Many reporters and interested followers of the story asked, "How could they forgive such a terrible, unprovoked act of violence against innocent lives?" The Amish culture closely follows the teachings of Jesus, who taught his followers to forgive one another, to place the needs of others before themselves, and to rest in the knowledge that God is still in control and can bring good out of any situation. Love and compassion toward others is to be life's theme. Vengeance and revenge is to be left to God.[8]

For a moment, blinded eyes were opened to the forgiveness modeled by fully devoted followers.

As you pray today at 9am or 9pm, praise God for the testimony given by these Amish mourners. Thank God for the forgiveness you've received and ask him to empower you to pass it on.

testimony

Good Morning - Day 22,

O ne of the statements dealing with speaking openly about God in this week's chapter says, "I will speak openly about God when I recognize God's work in my life" (*Imagine*, 58).

Yesterday afternoon I was out visiting prospects who have recently visited our services. At one home in Oneco, the lady who came to the door was the mother of the lady who visited the services. She explained to me that they had been shaken up quite a bit by a recent home invasion. Everyone in the house had been held at gunpoint. This had happened the week before their coming to church. She was thankful for God's protection in their lives. She spoke openly about God by recognizing God's work in that situation.

You may not have had such a traumatic experience as a home invasion recently, but if you pause long enough you should be able to recall/recognize recent work from God in your life. As you pray today at 9am or 9pm, praise God for his continuous presence in your life. Commit to be more conscience to share with others how great God is by how he is at work daily for you.

testimony

time

Good Morning - Day 23,

his week we move from T1, testimony, to T2, time. In one of this week's quiet times, the importance of spending time in God's Word is emphasized by looking at 2 Timothy 3:17. This verse encourages us to be in the Word to be "thoroughly equipped for every good work." That word *equipped* brought to my mind a conversation I had this past Wednesday.

That afternoon I visited with a young man serving time at Port Manatee. It was my first time to visit with him, so we had a lot to talk about. He had two items heavy on his mind: 1) containing his anger at the injustice he witnesses every day and 2) keeping his mind free from the guilt of his offense that he knows Jesus has forgiven. While we talked he mentioned that he knew he could do better about reading his Bible every day. He knew that when he read it he was better able to fend off Satan's attacks to his mind and spirit.

God turned my light bulb on. Ephesians 6 - that was his answer. That chapter talks about being equipped with God's armor to "stand against the devil's schemes." (Eph. 6:11) The very last verse describing the armor of God labels the word of God as the sword of the Spirit. As I made that connection for him, it looked like his light bulb came on. If he wants to experience victory against Satan, the key would be to spend time with God. It's similar to exercising - the more routine you have for exercising the stronger and more resilient you become. Thinking along those lines about spending time with God, the motivation suddenly changes from obligation to necessity.

So how's your equipping going? As you pray today at 9am or 9pm, thank God for his word. Commit to be faithful to spend time with him in order to be "thoroughly equipped for every good work" and able to "stand against the devil's schemes."

time

Good Morning - Day 24,

One of our recent quiet times took us to this verse from Psalm 5: *"In the morning, Lord, you hear my voice; in the morning I lay my requests before you and wait expectantly."* (verse 3, TNIV)

Here's a chance for me to be honest about two things:

1) I used to pride myself, and sometimes use it as an excuse for my attitude, that I am not a morning person. Through a couple of circumstances and disciplines I have come to believe that thinking was just a crutch to allow myself to be selfish. "I sleep until the last possible second" is an example of my poor excuse for not better disciplining my morning time.

2) I used to pride myself that I did my quiet times before going to bed rather than first thing in the morning. I didn't say this out loud to anyone, but I definitely practiced these thoughts: "I can do my quiet anytime of the day; those hyper-spiritual people who talk about meeting with God before doing anything else are just more morning people than I am. At least I spend time with God before I go to bed."

God starting correcting my stupidity (I can say that since I am talking about myself) about 12 years ago. My practices were nothing more than a reflection of my unwillingness to allow God to be Lord of my entire day. What I like about this verse is that David not only reveals his morning routine but also mentions two important actions. He said, "I lay my requests before you." I don't know what David's day planner looked like, but I imagine his roles of king, father, and husband gave him plenty of chances to have a lot on his plate for the day. What better routine to start your day with than to lay everything down before your Lord. The second action he mentions is "waiting expectantly." That is

time

my favorite part of the verse. Rather than rushing through his morning devotions, he waits on God to answer. This means taking time to pray and meditate, creating the mindset of expectation of God's work through the day ahead.

Make the most of your mornings. Spend unhurried moments with God. Receive refreshment for your soul. As you pray today at 9am or 9pm, lay your request before him and wait expectantly.

time

Good Morning - Day 25,

T he character for today's thought is Jezebel. You are probably wondering what good looking at her life will do you today. Well, in our chapter this week on craving, we read about five wrong cravings that come from unhealthy spiritual nutrition. I thought it would be good for a few days to look at some familiar characters with wrong cravings to see how things worked out for them. Jezebel, whose life was spoiled by malice, is first on the list.

"Malice is a desire to cause others pain and suffering because of our feelings about their behavior." (*Imagine*, 72) Jezebel, along with her unhealthy spiritual husband King Ahab (I chose to be nice in my description of him), probably illustrated more malice in her life than is recorded in the book of 1 Kings, but here's what we know. We know that she went after the prophet of God, Elijah, after he showed up her 450 false prophets of Baal on Mount Carmel. Actually since he killed all of them, it should have come as no surprise to him when Jezebel's messenger arrived saying, *"May the gods strike me and even kill me if by this time tomorrow I have not killed you just as you killed them."* (1 Kings 19:2, NLT) Her worshipping false gods led her to cause pain to the prophet of the God of Israel. The next example comes a couple of chapters later where she actually pulls off killing someone. Well, she didn't actually do it; she ordered someone to do it for her. Okay, well, it wasn't really for her; it was for her spineless husband Ahab (It's time to call it like it is). What did this person do? All he did was say no when Ahab tried to convince him to trade vineyards. Ahab sulked to Jezebel, and the rest is history (1 Kings 21). How did things work out for Ahab and Jezebel? Three years later, Ahab was killed in battle, and the dogs licked up his blood out of his chariot (1 Kings 22). Another twelve years later, Jezebel was thrown from a window

time

to her death, and dogs came and ate her body. Looks like it didn't pay to turn their backs on the God of Israel (2 Kings 9).

Now we may not let our spiritual nutrition get so far out of hand that we contrive to kill, but we can allow our desires to misguide us in dealing with others with whom we disagree. How 'bout that coworker that you just can't figure out how they keep getting promoted? Or that sibling that won't do their part in taking care of your ailing parent? Or that parent in the neighborhood that just doesn't see anything wrong with how their kid treats yours?

Check your heart today. Is there malice creeping in or that's well on its way to leading you to cause people to reject God? As you pray today at 9am or 9pm, let the Holy Spirit speak to you. Receive his words and get rid of any spoiled milk. Thank him for his forgiveness and the spiritual nutrition of love.

time

Good Morning - Day 26,

The character for today's thought is King Saul. He was the first person that came to my mind when I considered who struggled with the wrong craving of deceit. Deceit is the distortion of the truth to mislead others in an effort to harm them or to gain something personally (*Imagine*, 73). Here are a few examples of how this played out in Saul's life.

Saul acted deceptively with several people in his life. He tried to lead David to believe that he enjoyed having him around when in reality he was jealous of him and would have loved to see him dead. As for his own son Jonathan, who happened to be best friends with David, he plotted to pit Jonathan against David to satisfy his own desires. But the person he should have by all means known better than to deceive was Samuel, the prophet of God who appointed him as Israel's first king. The first instance was when he made excuses for breaking God's commands about offering sacrifices. He got tired of waiting on Samuel to show up to do the priestly function and decided to do it himself since he needed "the Lord's favor." For this Samuel told him, "Your kingdom will not endure" (1 Samuel 13). I believe 1 Samuel 15 records the saddest chapter in Saul's life. He blatantly disobeys God's instructions given to him by Samuel and then says to Samuel's face, "I have carried out the Lord's instructions." By the time Saul finally admitted his sin, it was too late.

time

*"Samuel said to him, 'The Lord has torn the kingdom of
Israel from you today and has given it to one of your
neighbors - to one better than you. He who is the Glory of
Israel does not lie or change his mind; for he is not a man,
that he should change his mind'...Until the day Samuel
died, he did not go to see Saul again, though Samuel
mourned for him. And the Lord was grieved that he had
made Saul king over Israel."* (15:28-29, 35)

We are tempted to feed on deceit usually to protect
ourselves. And have you noticed that once you've started it
tends to get a little easier. Saul definitely illustrated that,
but it led to his failure as a king, a father, and a friend. Are
you already saving a place on your plate for a helping of
deceit? Take it from Saul - it's best to let that bowl keep on
moving around the table.

As you pray today at 9am or 9pm, ask the Holy Spirit to
show you if you have been distorting the truth to others.
Commit to correct any misleadings and to begin exercising
a better diet of living out the truth.

time

Good Morning - Day 27,

So let's take a look at one more character who dabbled with some spoiled milk. David, known as a man after God's own heart, is well known in all walks of life for his adulterous act with another man's wife. Let's consider what role envy had in it and how it left lifelong tragedy for his family.

Envy is not being content and/or coveting what someone else has, whether it's possessions, position, or power (Imagine, 74). It appears from the first time David comes on the scene in 1 Samuel 16 until 2 Samuel 11 that he would prove to live a life pretty void of spoiled milk. The first two verses of that pivotal chapter, however, give us suggestions of why David fell. First, he shouldn't have been at home; according to verse 1, he normally would have been in battle. So he appears to be taking it easy - you might say he was being lazy. Well, his laziness left him susceptible to lust, which he gave in to after seeing Bathsheba bathing. He sent for her. He went after her. He lost sight that she wasn't his to have. He pulled rank. He had moved from laziness to lust to envy. It didn't end there. He plotted successfully to have her become his by having her husband killed. He wasn't content until he had what he wanted. The results? Their baby died. Chaos reigned in David's family for the duration of his life.

It might seem unfair that one adulterous act cost David so much. It might seem that way until you remember that God is completely void of sin. One sin - whether it's laziness,

time

lust, envy, slander, whatever - is all it takes to cause the spiritual diet to be tainted, to

cause separation from the Holy One of Israel. The great thing about David's story, unlike the stories of Jezebel and Saul, is when he was faced with his sin he truthfully repented. God's grace is enough to cover a multitude of sins, to correct our cravings.

For the last three days we've looked at three of the five sins Peter listed that can ruin one's spiritual nutrition. We realize there are many more, right? As you pray today at 9am or 9pm, open your heart to the Holy Spirit's examination for any spoiling sins. Say with David, *"Purify me from my sins, and I will be clean; wash me, and I will be whiter than snow. Oh, give me back my joy again; you have broken me--now let me rejoice...Restore to me the joy of your salvation and make me willing to obey you."* (Psalm 51:7-8, 12, NLT)

time

Good Morning - Day 28,

oday and tomorrow I'd like to take notice of two guys who figured out the best craving is for the right life. Today let's look at a character from our first week of quiet times - Zacchaeus.

Apparently, little Zacc didn't have a good reputation in Jericho. It didn't help that he collected taxes from his own people for the benefit of the Roman government who ruled Israel at this time. Tax collectors were known to be rich at other's expense. That's why the people labeled him a "notorious sinner." (Luke 19:7) But check out what he said to Jesus after spending some time with him: *"I will give half my wealth to the poor, Lord, and if I have cheated people on their taxes, I will give them back four times as much!"* Sounds to me like his craving changed. Because of that Jesus responded, *"Salvation has come to this home today."* (19:8-9, NLT) I'd say Zacchaeus was choosing the feel-good, blame-free, guilt-free, positive-influence life (Imagine, 77-78).

Zacchaeus's desire reminds me of a song released by Margaret Becker in 1998 called "Horses." Here are some of the lyrics:

> Last night I dreamed of horses coming for my soul
> Taking me to places I wasn't ready yet to go
>
> Last night I dreamed of silence, the silence that I keep

time

All the things I could've said; well, they stole away
my sleep

I need to remember the horses will come
I need to remember how quickly they run

I want no regrets when the horses come for me
I cannot forget that the horses come for me

I need to remember You're always with me
I need to remember You're the reason I breathe[9]

As you pray today at 9am or 9pm, thank God for the power
to change your cravings. Thank him for the remembrance
that he's always with you to help you live the life he has for
you.

time

Good Morning - Day 29,

I don't know if there is a clearer example in the Bible of someone's cravings changing than Paul. Apparently his reputation as a persecutor of Christians was well known. That seems why Ananias, after being asked to go help Paul receive his sight after being blinded by God's light, pretty much replied, "Are you serious? I can't believe we are talking about the same person." The great change that had come over him baffled even the Jews in Damascus. Their astonishment came from watching him grow "more and more powerful by proving that Jesus is the Christ." (Acts 9:22)

The encouragement that we can draw from Paul's life is that the craving change is possible for anyone. Regardless of the depth of your bad craving, God can change it. Regardless of your past history or present indulgence, God is willing to help you overcome that craving and give you a new diet. Another great illustration of Paul's life is how God used who he was. His zealous scholarship did not go to waste. His transformation into a fully devoted follower allowed him to truthfully say, *"For to me, to live is Christ and to die is gain."* (Phil. 1:21) His cravings had to have been right in order to make that declaration.

Is Satan telling you it just isn't possible to change that craving or that God won't forgive you for that indulgence? As you pray today at 9am or 9pm, claim the truth that with God all is possible. Thank him for blinding you with his truth and starting the craving change in your life. Ask him to make it obvious to people that you belong to him.

time

Good Morning - Day 30,

O ur chapter title for this week is "The Disciplines: Imagine a life that manages its opportunities." The word *discipline* reminded me of a blog entry I made a few months back. Here's some of that entry:

> Yesterday I was asked if I ever struggle keeping up with the daily routine of spending time with God through Bible reading or any other means of "quiet time." My immediate response was, "Of course. Who doesn't?"

> I say that because I believe it. I would expect that we all go through ups and downs, highs and lows, seasons of hunger and complacency, and on and on you can go with the comparisons. Why is this? Because we are human. We still are drawn to our natural desires. That's why pursuing a godly life, pursuing daily habits that transform us into our maker's image are called disciplines.

> I compare it to any activity you wish to become better at. For me, one of those is running. I guarantee you that I don't always look forward to jumping out of bed in the morning to hit the pavement. Do you know how hot it is in Florida in July at 8am? Your body's natural desire is to say, "Excuse me! Why did you just walk out of the air-conditioned comfort of the indoors?" It takes discipline (work) to say to myself, "Get up! This is what you must do to improve. I bet Ryan Hall (Olympic athlete) isn't still in bed. Lace it up." That's my comparison to the struggle.

> So what do you do about it? The great thing to me is you have lots of options to keep the discipline going and

time

probably even invigorating. Maybe you start reading some entries online. Maybe you supplement your reading with writings of other authors in books or magazines. Maybe you have an accountability/mentor/mentee relationship that allows you to walk together with someone, challenge each other. Maybe you add the aspect of journaling. Maybe you focus on reading about a particular subject rather than following a regiment of reading a certain amount of chapters every day or following a certain schedule. Maybe you read the same Biblical book several times looking at it from various angles - who it was written to, how it relates to you/the church today. Maybe you forego reading and do more praying. Maybe you incorporate music into your discipline in some fashion. Maybe you incorporate more true "quiet time" by being silent and letting God speak and you listen.

You see what I mean? There are lots of "maybes." For me, the trick is discerning that I am actually struggling and figuring out why and then finding the solution. *I like to view those times as God desiring to add some spice to the conversation.* That's part of having a relationship, right?

Enjoy your discipline today!

As you pray today at 9am or 9pm, thank God for the opportunities he has given you to manage. Commit to be honest this week as you respond to his prompting as to how well you are managing them and how you could improve.

time

Good Morning - Day 31,

I'd like you to meet Tom White. Tom is a 47-year-old country doctor in Buena Vista, Colorado. Last November he faced a choice. It wasn't life or death. It was life or better life. Due to a motorcycle accident in his 20s, he had a degenerative condition in his left leg. Over the years he'd joked about getting his gimpy leg cut off. "When this thing doesn't serve me anymore," he'd tell his wife Tammy, "I'm going to get it amputated. Get a prosthesis." That's exactly what he did on November 27, 2007. It took just 22 minutes to lose the lower leg.

Why would he do this? To get back to who he used to be. Who he used to be was an elite collegiate track athlete. In 1977, Tom won the New Mexico cross-country state championship. In his second and third years in college, he and his teammates won the national team title championship. By the spring of his junior year, Tom had run a 4:02 mile and looked to vie for the individual title in the national cross-country championships the next fall. Then the accident happened. Now with his natural leg some 20 years later, he faced a future without running or hiking. Doing these pursuits gave him the sense of his core identity. As a doctor, Tom knows that 3,500 amputations are performed in the U.S. every week. The majority of these are for patients who have no choice due to diabetes, smoking, trauma, heart disease, cancer, obesity, or other ailments. "That's part of the reason I'm doing this," he said. "So I can say to my patients, 'Hey look at me, I've only got one good leg and I'm out there running, biking, staying active. You can do this.'" And he's proved it. Just

time

seven months after his surgery, learning to walk for the third time in his life and this time with a prothesis, he ran a 10-k. It was like a scent from childhood. That's what he missed the most, all those years. That's what he gave his left leg to get back again.[10]

In managing our opportunities for a disciplined life, we have to check our desires - make sure they are right. Is there something in your life that you need to give up in order to better your chances for living better? Maybe something that is taking up too much of your time? Or something that is hampering the work of the Holy Spirit in your life? Or something that just simply needs to be cut off? Before you pray today at 9am or 9pm, consider your answers to those questions. Ask God for the wisdom and discipline to make the right choices that will lead to the life he has for you.

time

Good Morning - Day 32,

his week's chapter makes quite a few references to Solomon and his wisdom for following God. He wrote the book of Ecclesiastes which is a study of finding purpose in life. He describes how certain paths in life lead to emptiness. This emptiness is the result of a life without God. As we think about managing our lives, how can we possible consider doing so without God? That's what leads Solomon to conclude at the end of Ecclesiastes, *"Fear God and keep his commandments, for this is the whole duty of man."* (12:13)

Reading this week's chapter reminded me of the lyrics to the hymn "Take Time to be Holy." Here's a little bit of the story behind this song:

> This hymn is a good example of the Lord making more of our work than we could have expected. The man who wrote the words to "Take Time to Be Holy" was neither a pastor nor a songwriter. William Longstaff was an English businessman — a Christian layman who took his faith seriously. Hearing a sermon on the text, "Be ye holy, for I am holy," Longstaff was inspired to write a poem, "Take Time to Be Holy." Being a good businessman, Longstaff had a practical mind. That is reflected in this hymn, which offers many practical suggestions for becoming holy.
> — He says, *"Take time to be holy,"* which reflects his understanding that holiness, like every virtue,

time

requires time and attention to develop it.

— He says, *"Speak oft with the Lord,"* reflecting his personal experience that prayer deepens faith.

— He says, *"Take time to be holy, Be calm in your soul; Each thought and each motive, Beneath His control,"* telling us that we can face adversity calmly if we look to Christ for guidance.

Longstaff managed to get his poem published in a Christian newspaper, but that was the end of it — or so it seemed. But as it turned out, George Stebbins, a Christian musician, had seen the poem and had clipped and filed it. Years later, needing a hymn on the subject of holy living, he remembered the poem and set it to music. It has been a favorite now for more than a century. I don't know whether Longstaff ever knew that Stebbins had set his poem to music. I don't know that he ever heard it sung. I know only that he felt called to write the poem — and that God did the rest. When we do something good — something for God — we might never know the full measure of good that we have accomplished. We can only know that God will take what we offer, great or small, and make of it a treasure.[11]

As you pray today at 9am or 9pm, thank God for being available to help you manage life.   Ask him to reveal to you anything that needs better managing for this day's living.

time

Good Morning - Day 33,

This week's chapter contains four great questions we should ask ourselves when making decisions. One of these is "what does God want?" One of the best examples of someone asking this question in the Bible comes from one of the Judges, Gideon.

From the very first words out of his mouth recorded in scripture, this is what Gideon has on his mind. *"Why has all this happened...where are all the miracles our ancestors told us about?"* My interpretation of that is, "What are you up to, God?" Once Gideon gets it loud and clear that the man he is talking with is actually the Angel of the Lord, his questions shift. His fears and doubts cause him to continue to challenge God's promise, *"I will be with you. And you will destroy the Midianites as if you were fighting against one man."* God remains patient and grants Gideon enough grace to solidify his faith so he could carry out exactly what God wanted. (Judges 6-8, NLT)

When we seek God's face during questioning times, it's natural to ask him, "What's up?" When we are more concerned about his accomplishing what he wants, we are well on the way to fulfilling our part and to making a wise decision. As you pray today at 9am or 9pm, thank God for always being at work on your behalf. Commit to growing in your discipline to ask first what he wants before declaring what you want.

time

Good Morning - Day 34,

I'd like to continue today looking at another one of the questions we should ask when making decisions. After asking what God wants, we should ask ourselves if we are willing to do what God wants. Jesus had a conversation with one young man who definitely had to face that very same question.

Jesus was teaching, as recorded for us in Matthew 19, when he was asked by this young man, *"What good deed must I do to have eternal life?"* Jesus answered, but the young man felt like he had already accomplished the answer. So then he asked, "What else must I do?" Here's how Jesus replied: *"If you want to be perfect, go and sell all your possessions and give the money to the poor, and you will have treasure in heaven. Then come, follow me."* (verse 21, NLT) Well, that's where the conversation ended. The young man went away sad still clinging to his possessions and still hopeless regarding eternal life. His answer to the question "do I want to do what God wants" was "No."

Sad story. And we both know that story is repeated every day in lives. And, if we are honest, we sometimes say no to what God wants also. As you pray today at 9am or 9pm, lift up those you know that are seeking eternal life. Ask the Holy Spirit to soften their hearts in order that they will want what God wants. As for your heart, seek to be honest with God about what he is asking you to do. If you have been saying no, let the Holy Spirit work in you to change your answer.

time

Good Morning - Day 35,

O ur chapter this week presents six types of lives for us to pursue in our efforts to achieve a life of purpose. One of these is the Honest Life = the Fair Life. We were challenged with the question, "Do you treat people fairly, or do you play favorites? If you play favorites, why do you do so?"

When you hear the word "*favorite*," you hear it used in the context of various things like food (my favorite candy is tootsie rolls), drinks (my favorite soda is root beer - A&W or Barqs), or sports teams (my teams: NFL=Jaguars, MLB=Cardinals, College FB=the Crimson Tide of Alabama). The thought of favorites in the context of people may or may not be the same idea; I guess it depends on how far we go with our favoritism. Some fans of other teams are great to be around; they understand the boundaries of friendly competition. Other fans are out of control - fighting in the stands, burning buses, or turning over police cars.

So how does this compare to our dealings with one another on a daily basis? Having favorites plays out in our families, for one thing. Take for example the parenting skills of Isaac and Rebecca displayed in Genesis 25-27. They pretty much helped their twins, Esau and Jacob, become the rivals God predicted they would be (Gen. 25:23). The lies and deception leading to stealing and desires to murder seemed to be aided by the favoritism of mom and dad. Favoritism also plays out in the workplace.

time

Just listen to the news today, right? Another example of favoritism that cuts more to the heart is given to us in Luke 10 in the story of the Good Samaritan. Jesus told this story in reply to the question, "Who is

my neighbor?" The obvious choice of who was the best neighbor to the traveler was "the one who showed him mercy." There was no favoritism in the Samaritan's heart. Someone was in need. He chose to show mercy.

So at the end of the ballgame, or even in the third quarter when your team is getting crushed, is it worth all the angst? When things don't go as you'd like with personnel at work, is it worth starting rumors or becoming slanderous? And how 'bout that neighbor across the street who hasn't been the friendliest to your family, but today you see they can't get their car started? Is it okay to ignore them when your trunk contains the jumper cables they need? As you pray today at 9am or 9pm, ask God to seek your heart for any unfair treatment of others. If necessary, commit to setting things right with them. Also, thank God for his mercy available to both you and your neighbor.

time

Good Morning - Day 36,

The two disciplines this week's chapter looked at were prayer and study. In the acrostic for study, we touched on the element of understanding - taking time to gain more instruction if I don't understand what God's Word says to me. The first person in the Bible that came to my mind when I read that description was Nicodemus.

Remember him from John 3? He was the Pharisee that sought out Jesus for a private conversation. Here are the whopping 5 sentences recorded by John that Nicodemus said in that conversation:

"Rabbi, we know you are a teacher who has come from God. For no one could perform the miraculous signs you are doing if God were not with him...How can a man be born when he is old? Surely he cannot enter a second time into his mother's womb to be born!...How can this be?"

I can picture Jesus smiling recognizing that Nicodemus was seeking understanding. He may have been fearful of being exposed for trying to connect with Jesus, but he was still seeking understanding. He was attracted by Jesus' character and miracles. Eventually he believed. We see him appear again in Jesus' story in John 7, speaking up for Jesus, and 19, joining Joseph of Arimathea in burying Jesus. One great truth you can take from his story is that God will not hide himself from those who seek him. You may not "get it" right away, but what can you expect?

time

You're a finite being trying to understand the infinite God of the universe. And isn't it worth it?

As you pray today at 9am or 9pm, thank God for allowing you the opportunity to know him, to spend time with him, to seek understanding. Praise him for his greatness and commit to pursue knowing him better and better.

time

talents

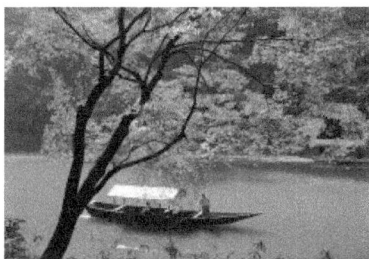

Good Morning - Day 37,

This week's chapter subtitle is "imagine a life that exercises concern for others." I was watching the news on Thursday evening and saw a story of a piano prodigy who gave a great illustration of this kind of life.

His name is Marc Yu. Marc is nine years old and lives in Pasadena. When he was 3, Marc played Beethoven at his first concert and 6 years later he is performing at Albert Hall in London. "I want to achieve incredible things. That's why I practice a lot," Marc said. Which, of course, is how you get to Carnegie Hall. He's playing there next year. These facts are great and remarkable, but the illustration of concern for others was what caught my attention. In Mobile, Ala., on his mission to turn children on to classics, he performed benefit concerts, raising $680,000 for victims of the Szechwan earthquake. Do you remember being 9? Was it even on your radar to achieve something like this? It sure wasn't on mine. Of course, God has given Marc a tool to work with. I'm glad - and I'm sure God is - that he isn't keeping it to himself.[12]

As you pray today at 9am or 9pm, take a moment to let God show you what tools he have given you to exercise concern for others. Thank him for them. Commit to follow his lead in using those tools.

talents

Good Morning - Day 38,

Here's a quote from chapter 6 of our Imagine book: "People don't buy in to God's love until they experience it." (Imagine, 112) The paragraph goes on to illustrate how we experience life through our senses. That's what I'd like to focus on the next few days - illustrations of God's love channeled through our senses. Let's start with sight.

The Bible is full of illustrations for us to see God's love. Creation began it all. Noah saw a rainbow. Abraham saw a ram. The Israelites saw the walls of Jericho fall. Their first king and his army saw a shepherd kill a giant with a slingshot. Nebuchadnezzar saw four men walking in a furnace. Daniel saw hungry lions ignore him. The shepherds and wise men saw God come to them in a manger. Many turned to Jesus after seeing him heal, raise the dead, and multiply food. As if that wasn't enough, the best illustration wasn't seen until the cross. Once you experience the cross, God's love takes on a whole new look, another dimension you've yet to witness. This explains the two thieves' reactions to the event. One saw a way out of his predicament; the other saw that he was the predicament. The love evident by Jesus' sacrifice reveals who we are and who he longs to be for us. With that view, we can all echo with the soldier that day, "Surely he is the Son of God."

As you pray today at 9am or 9pm, take a moment to look around for evidences of God's love. Thank him for eyes to see his abundant love. Ask him to prepare the way for others to see that love through you.

talents

Good Morning - Day 39,

P am Leo in her comprehensive article on the need for infant touching and massage (*"Reach Out and Touch Someone: Massage in Schools"*) reviews studies showing that humans--especially at birth--need to be touched. Pam writes: 'Touch is one of our basic needs. As early as the 7th week of pregnancy, a baby reacts to touch. Touch is the earliest sense to develop and the last one to leave us at the end of life. Studies show that both people and animals develop very slowly and even die if they are denied touch...In the first two years of life 80% of a baby's brain growth is occurring. Babies who receive abundant touch will be more likely to reach the upper limits of their intellectual potential. Studies show that the brain of a child develops 20-30% more if they have received massage or touch often compared to children who have not.' Pam also points out in her article that humans touching and massaging infants and children also personally benefit. Touch is clearly a built-in sense that is necessary for human life."[13]

Of all people I would think that Jesus understood the necessity of touch. When I think about how he illustrated his love through touch, I immediately go to his miracles by which touch was the avenue of healing. He touched blinded eyes. He touched dead bodies. Once a lady touched his robe and he declared, "Your faith has healed you." But I believe the best picture of his love through

talents

touch was the miracle of healing the man with leprosy in Matthew 8. By law, like all other lepers he had been separated from society. So the very thought and follow through to intentionally touch him sent an incredible message. Here's Max Lucado's portrait of what this leper may have thought:

> "He stopped and looked in my direction as did dozens of others. Their panic I'd seen a thousand times. His compassion, however, I'd never beheld. Everyone stepped back except him. He stepped toward me. *Toward me.* Had he healed me with a word, I would have been thrilled. Had he cured me with a prayer, I would have rejoiced. But he wasn't satisfied with speaking to me. He drew near to me. He touched me...I will never forget the one who dared to touch me. He could have healed me with a word. But he wanted to do more than heal me. He wanted to honor me, to validate me, to christen me. Imagine that...unworthy of the touch of a man, yet worthy of the touch of God."[14]

So who in your world needs touching? The son of a drunk? A divorcee? The unemployed? An unmarried mother? The depressed? The terminally ill? The handicapped? As you pray today at 9am or 9pm, take a moment to consider someone to touch today with God's love. Follow his lead as you give your hand to him.

talents

Good Morning - Day 40,

Hearing a reminder that God loves us can bring warmth into coldness and hope into despair. When I think of the joy of realizing God's love for us, it makes me think of the song entitled "His Eye is on the Sparrow." I'd never heard the story behind that song, so I looked it up. Here's the story I found written by the song's author, Civilla Martin:

> Early in the spring of 1905, my husband and I were sojourning in Elmira, New York. We contracted a deep friendship for a couple by the name of Mr. and Mrs. Doolittle—true saints of God. Mrs. Doolittle had been bedridden for nigh twenty years. Her husband was an incurable cripple who had to propel himself to and from his business in a wheel chair. Despite their afflictions, they lived happy Christian lives, bringing inspiration and comfort to all who knew them. One day while we were visiting with the Doolittles, my husband commented on their bright hopefulness and asked them for the secret of it. Mrs. Doolittle's reply was simple: "His eye is on the sparrow, and I know He watches me." The beauty of this simple expression of boundless faith gripped the hearts and fired the imagination of Dr. Martin and me. The hymn "His Eye Is on the Sparrow" was the outcome of that experience.
> The next day she mailed the poem to Charles Gabriel, who supplied the music. Singer Ethel Waters so loved this song that she used its name as the title for her autobiography.

talents

Why should I feel discouraged, why should the shadows come,
Why should my heart be lonely, and long for heaven and home,

When Jesus is my portion? My constant friend is He:
His eye is on the sparrow, and I know He watches me;
His eye is on the sparrow, and I know He watches me.

Refrain
I sing because I'm happy, I sing because I'm free,
For His eye is on the sparrow, and I know He watches me.

"Let not your heart be troubled," His tender word I hear,
And resting on His goodness, I lose my doubts and fears;
Though by the path He leadeth, but one step I may see;
His eye is on the sparrow, and I know He watches me;
His eye is on the sparrow, and I know He watches me.

Refrain

Whenever I am tempted, whenever clouds arise,
When songs give place to sighing, when hope within me dies,
I draw the closer to Him, from care He sets me free;
His eye is on the sparrow, and I know He watches me;
His eye is on the sparrow, and I know He watches me.

Refrain[15]

As you pray today at 9am or 9pm, thank God for voices, written or spoken, who share his love. Commit to be his voice to someone today.

talents

Good Morning - Day 41,

There's a story in 2 Kings about a well-to-do woman who took care of a prophet by feeding him whenever he stopped by their home. Her hospitality was so strong and he apparently ended up there so much that she urged her husband to build an additional room to their home just for this prophet, Elisha. The story doesn't reveal any motive on this couple's part but simply to meet a need. Through them Elisha tasted the love of his God.

The story doesn't end there, though. Elisha prophesied to the woman that, in spite of her husband's age, she would have a son. This happened, but several years later her son died. The mother's response is recorded in chapter 4:21-37. She took her son's dead body and laid him on the bed in the room of the prophet. She then traveled to the city where Elisha was and told him what had happened. With God's power, Elisha traveled back to the boy and was able to bring him back to life. A relationship that had started over the provision of physical food was deepened by the provision of physical life. Brings a whole new dimension to the verse, *"Taste and see that the Lord is good."* (Psalm 34:8)

As you pray today at 9am or 9pm, thank God for those who have given you a taste of his love through their hospitality. Maybe you can think of someone with whom you can share that love in a similar way - give them a gift card, take them to lunch, bake them a pie, or have them over for dinner. Who knows what may be down the road in your relationship just because you gave them a little taste of God's love.

talents

Good Morning - Day 42,

As I was thinking about this last scent to write about - smell - I thought of this verse from 2 Corinthians. It reads, *"Thanks be to God who...uses us to spread the aroma of the knowledge of him everywhere."* (2:14, TNIV) Pretty neat thought - that we can spread his aroma.

When you think of the smell of clean, what comes to mind? Lysol? Pinesol? Mr. Clean? Snuggles? Bounce? Dawn? What comes to mind for me these days is Downy. The last bottle of Tide I bought has a "touch of Downy" added. So I am experiencing a new smell when I am dressing these days. Well, whatever that scent is that comes to mind for you, let me draw a comparison. What is it like being around a group of believers compared to being around a group of nonbelievers? Thinking in terms of cleanliness, does that bring a different sensation to your nose? Now I'm not saying unsaved people categorically smell, but would you agree there is a sense of wholesomeness, purity, or cleanliness with believers that just doesn't come off as well in different circles? That's what comes to mind when I read this verse from Paul. So the personal question for us today is, when others are around me what fragrance am I giving off? Might sound funny, but take a whiff and see what you think.

As you pray today at 9am or 9pm, ask God how you "smell" today. If you are a little stinky, ask him to clean you up, get rid of that odor that's keeping you from spreading his aroma. For a practical idea of spreading his aroma, see if he leads you to help someone clean up something today - like their house or a room in it, their yard, their office, or their vehicle. Go ahead and spray a little good smelling stuff wherever you go today.

talents

Good Morning - Day 43,

In our last thought for this week that has focused on "exercising concern for others," I thought I'd give an example from David's life that illustrated this quote from page 116 in our chapter:

"The heart is where our spirit comes in. The spirit that motivates us drives our service, whether for self or others. We live to please the spirit that's in control. We are to follow God's Spirit." (*Imagine*)

There is an incredible example of this in David's story before he becomes king. Do you remember the period where David was basically running for his life because of the anger of King Saul? In one scene, Saul comes into a cave to "take care of business" and is completely unaware that David is hiding out in that very cave. David's men urge him to take revenge on Saul and this is where the story gets really interesting. Let's pick it up in verse 4 of 1 Samuel 24:

4 The men said, "This is the day the LORD spoke of when he said to you, 'I will give your enemy into your hands for you to deal with as you wish.' " Then David crept up unnoticed and cut off a corner of Saul's robe.

5 Afterward, David was conscience-stricken for having cut off a corner of his robe. 6 He said to his men, "The LORD forbid that I should do such a thing to my master, the LORD's anointed, or lay my hand on him; for he is the anointed of the LORD." 7 With these words David sharply

talents

rebuked his men and did not allow them to attack Saul. And Saul left the cave and went his way.

8 Then David went out of the cave and called out to Saul, "My lord the king!" When Saul looked behind him, David bowed down and prostrated himself with his face to the ground. 9 He said to Saul, "Why do you listen when men say, 'David is bent on harming you'? 10 This day you have seen with your own eyes how the LORD delivered you into my hands in the cave. Some urged me to kill you, but I spared you; I said, 'I will not lay my hand on my lord, because he is the LORD's anointed.' 11 See, my father, look at this piece of your robe in my hand! I cut off the corner of your robe but did not kill you. See that there is nothing in my hand to indicate that I am guilty of wrongdoing or rebellion. I have not wronged you, but you are hunting me down to take my life. 12 May the LORD judge between you and me. And may the LORD avenge the wrongs you have done to me, but my hand will not touch you. 13 As the old saying goes, 'From evildoers come evil deeds,' so my hand will not touch you.

14 "Against whom has the king of Israel come out? Whom are you pursuing? A dead dog? A flea? 15 May the LORD be our judge and decide between us. May he consider my cause and uphold it; may he vindicate me by delivering me from your hand."

16 When David finished saying this, Saul asked, "Is that your voice, David my son?" And he wept aloud. 17 "You are more righteous than I," he said. "You have treated me well, but I have treated you badly. 18 You have just now told me about the good you did to me; the LORD delivered

talents

me into your hands, but you did not kill me. 19 When a man finds his enemy, does he let him get away unharmed? May the LORD reward you well for the way you treated me today.

Pretty incredible, right? That is one man following the right spirit. David's actions led Saul to admit, "You are more righteous than I." David exercised more concern for following his Lord which directly impacted his concern for Saul, the very man who wanted him dead.

More than likely, you aren't worried about someone trying to kill you today. But Satan definitely wants you to think serving yourself is of utmost importance whenever you are feeling attacked. As you pray today at 9am or 9pm, ask God to check your spirit. If you are battling exercising more concern for yourself than others, yield that battle to his spirit. Before acting in the wrong spirit, try cutting off a corner of your attacker's robe and let God take care of the rest.

talents

Good Morning - Day 44,

O ur second week on the "T" of talents challenges us to engage the community. A few weeks ago on my blog I included a link to a video piece about Tom Cousins I had seen on TV. Reading the opening story in our chapter this week about Terry Lane from Jacksonville reminded me of Tom's story. Here's my blog entry:

> This afternoon I saw this video clip while watching golf on NBC. It features Tom Cousins, an Atlanta realtor who took on changing the future of a horrible community. 60% of people living in this community lived on welfare. It was called Little Vietnam because of a crime rate 18 times the national average. The change is spectacular. Watch the video and see the new EastLake and the lives that have been changed. Why? In Cousins' words, "There but for the grace of God go I."[16]

As you pray today at 9am or 9pm, ask God to use this week's study to give you clarity. If you are already engaged in the community, ask God to continue to guide you in that engagement. If you aren't engaged, commit to follow God's leading in doing what he has "prepared in advance for you to do."

talents

Good Morning - Day 45,

One of the reminders to us in our chapter this week is that God created us for a task. Just Sunday morning I was talking with a mom in the Fruitstand (Woodland bookstore) about her daughter who started MCC this fall. She told me that since she was a young girl her daughter has always known that she wanted to study marine biology. There's never been a question, and that is exactly the road she is going down for her studies. Amazing how obvious some of our tasks are God-given, isn't it?

I'd like to give you a great illustration of how one man is serving others using what God created him to do. His name is David Puckett. I came across his story on CNN the other day while eating lunch. CNN is honoring 10 people who they have labeled heroes for 2008. Here's a portion of David's story from CNN's website:

> Since November 2000, the certified, licensed prosthetist/orthotist from Savannah, Georgia, has been providing artificial limbs, orthopedic braces and ongoing care to hundreds in need in the communities of Mexico's Yucatan Peninsula and Chiapas -- free of charge.
> "When someone loses a limb they immediately know what they've lost," says Puckett. "The goal is to restore the healthy self image again so that that person can see themselves whole."
> Puckett first connected with the Yucatan people while volunteering on a mission there as a teenager. Struck by the overwhelming poverty and the physical challenges he saw people facing in the rural communities, Puckett vowed to return and make a difference there.
> "When I finally got into the field of orthotics and prosthetics, I said, 'Ah-ha. Now, I know what I can do.' "
> His nonprofit, PIPO Missions: Limbs and Braces to Mexico,

talents

collects donated, used orthopedic braces and artificial limbs in the United States and crafts new ones from their recycled components. On average, Puckett makes a six-day trip every two months to distribute the custom prosthetics and braces, while also providing ongoing care.

Over the course of his 41 trips to the region, Puckett has helped more than 420 individuals. For Puckett, each trip demonstrates the immeasurable impact he is making on people's lives. Stories of previously unimagined independence, confidence and employment greet him from clinical waiting areas, often along with offerings of food, livestock and friendship. When his group helps one person, Puckett explains, it has an effect on an entire community.

"It opens a whole other door for many of these folks to experience the world in a way in which they've never even dreamt of," says Puckett. "And the world has an opportunity to greet them, accept them and welcome them back into society. So, it's a double blessing."

In between trips, Puckett also spends time soliciting the aid of surgeons, as he frequently encounters physical conditions that require surgery before prosthetic help can be successfully administered.

"If we had a surgeon here, we could see eight to 10 patients in a weekend and change their lives forever," he says. "It's tough for people to make the choice to give up time with their families and a portion of their income to extend themselves in this way. But, take it from me, the more we give, the more we get."[17]

As you pray today at 9am or 9pm, thank God for what he has given you to use to give to others. Commit to follow through with fulfilling the task he created for you. While you're praying, take a moment to lift up David and his work in Mexico.

talents

Good Morning - Day 46,

This email may come across as more than you wanted to know, but I'd like to share what I got from my reading just now. It comes from quiet time week 6 day 5.

All my life I've had perfectionistic tendencies. In elementary school I worked hard to earn as many academic awards that I could every year. If I feel strongly about a certain task, I give it all I've got. I was valedictorian of my high school graduating class, made the dean's list every semester in college - yada, yada, yada. My major in music education was an interesting challenge for me, though, because of these tendencies. Lack of a solid technical piano background limited my abilities to be the best in the class - a good lesson in humility to learn.

Now as I serve in ministry I have another slant to this challenge. You've probably heard of that 80/20 rule - 20 percent of the people do 80 percent of the work. I don't mind being part of the 20. I tend not to judge the other 80; if anything I may be rougher on the other 20. I take a different look at it. I actually find myself frustrated that God doesn't give me more to do, like I haven't reached my full potential. A little twisted, eh? Funny how overachievers have to be told to take it easy while underachievers have to continuously be kicked in the derriere. At times though, I believe we all need a little bit of both.

talents

So what in the world does this have to do with Ephesians 4:32-5:2? I don't see it anywhere in those verses that we are asked to save the world all by ourselves. God just says, "Hey, whatever you are doing, just imitate me. Just do your job well and that is enough. It actually pleases me that you are doing what I've asked you to do and you're doing your best to do it like I would. I know you're not perfect, but I'm thrilled that you are keeping on and trying hard." You might say the message I got from God today was straight through the megaphone, "John, atta boy. Now chill out."

I'm not sure what you may be getting from these thoughts, but here is my encouragement to you today. As you pray today at 9am or 9pm, ask God what he thinks of your recent service to him and others. More than likely you already know, but it is good to give him a chance to tell you. Also, thank him for his son's example of sacrifice and love. Commit to strive to be more like him and thus to be "a pleasing aroma to God."

talents

Good Morning - Day 47,

This week's chapter reminds us that we need to check our motivations for doing what God asks of us. "If we have the wrong motivation, we won't accomplish our purpose." (*Imagine*, 125)

A couple of examples from the New Testament come to mind for me when thinking of people with wrong motivations:

I'm not sure I'll ever get a good grasp on the motivations of Judas. Scripture just doesn't give me enough to go on to see how a man accepts the call to travel with Jesus, watches him perform miracles, hears his incredible teaching, eats and sleeps with his entourage, yet somehow gets motivated to betray him. The implications point to money and greed, but that's just a guess. Whatever it was, it led Judas to kill himself in the end. Hardly what I imagine God had in store for the purpose of his life.

Now the next example made it pretty obvious what their motivations were. The Pharisees, chief priests, and elders of the people could have a whole thesaurus devoted to them, it seems. That thesaurus could probably be based on just one word - *pride*. Their motivations had gotten so far away from God's intentions that they couldn't see the wrong in their perceived right. All the "good" they were doing, according to Jesus, was hypocritical. They were nothing more than blind guides, fools, and snakes (Matthew 23). Ouch! I don't know about you, but I'm not interested in the

talents

son of God having to slap me with the reality that my motivations are so screwed up that he has to get that righteously angry with me.

Let's face it, though. Sometimes our motivations need realignment. As you pray today at 9am or 9pm, ask God to check your heart's motivations. Confess and get rid of the wrong ones. Thank him for reminding you of the right ones.

talents

Good Morning - Day 48,

In the comments about how we do the works of our God-given purpose, our chapter makes a comparison with the work of mechanics. When we do good works, "we're like good mechanics who actually fix what's broken." (*Imagine*, 126)

A clear example of this is displayed through the life of Nehemiah. Nehemiah got news that made him cry. The exiles who had returned from Persia nearly a hundred years earlier had yet to rebuild the city walls of Jerusalem. Nehemiah, still in Persia, was moved to fix the problem. He got permission from the king and went back to lead the completion of this work in 52 days - less than 2 months on a job that hadn't been completed for a century. His work involved praying, fasting, bringing order, leading by example, and establishing accountability. This work allowed the city to reestablish a measure of security against her enemies that had been missing for years. A transformation happened when one man followed through to obediently fix what was broken.

Think about your world. Anything broken? Anything unsecure? Attitude, family relationships, perspective, view of God? As you pray today at 9am or 9pm, ask God to break your heart over it and to provide you with the courage and wisdom to fix that broken item in your world. Thank him for opening your eyes to the problem and for giving you the tools to be a good mechanic.

talents

Good Morning - Day 49,

O n Day 45 we looked at David from Savannah who is illustrating doing a task he was created to do. I want to remind you of a story from 2 Kings 5 that further illustrates this truth from our chapter: "You're important because God created your job for you, not for someone else. He did it for you." (*Imagine*, 126) Here are the first 4 verses of this chapter. Pay attention to the young girl.

1 Now Naaman was commander of the army of the king of Aram. He was a great man in the sight of his master and highly regarded, because through him the LORD had given victory to Aram. He was a valiant soldier, but he had leprosy.
2 Now bands from Aram had gone out and had taken captive a young girl from Israel, and she served Naaman's wife.
3 She said to her mistress, "If only my master would see the prophet who is in Samaria! He would cure him of his leprosy."
4 Naaman went to his master and told him what the girl from Israel had said.

That's it. That's all we hear about this little girl. But I think it's enough. It's enough because she did her job. When you read the rest of the story, you see how Naaman, after quite a hullabaloo, does end up being healed of his leprosy. This little girl could have had every reason in the world to keep the good news to herself. Apparently she knew better than to be that selfish. In spite of being captive, in spite of

talents

serving strangers, in spite of being young, in spite of being a girl, in spite of being a foreigner, in spite of anything else that could have kept her mouth shut, she did something that only she could have done. The story doesn't record it, but I imagine that God allowed her to know how happy he was that she did exactly what he created her to do.

As you pray today at 9am or 9pm, thank God for creating you with and for a purpose. Ask him to remove the "in spite of's" from your heart so you can fulfill and be fulfilled doing that purpose.

talents

Good Morning - Day 50,

ere's a great statement of encouragement: "If we don't work, God doesn't throw us out of the body and replace us...He keeps doing things in our lives to encourage us to change our motivation by changing our power source. He does so in an effort to bring our service back to life." (*Imagine*, 127) There's not a clearer picture of this in the Bible than the life of Samson found in Judges 13-16.

Verse 5 of chapter 13 reveals what Samson's task was to be: "He will begin the deliverance of Israel from the hands of the Philistines." Interesting. Why? Because when we think about what sticks in our minds from his story, deliverance from the Philistines is probably not at the forefront. You might think more about Samson along these lines: "What a jokster! He seemed to just live for the moment. It would catch up with him, then he'd do some incredible thing like kill 1,000 men with a donkey's jawbone to even the score. And his weakness for women. Can you imagine what he could have done if he'd just stayed faithful to God more than not?" And your thoughts are legitimate. But let's consider the end of his life.

The last eleven verses of chapter 16 show the result of his humbling. Once his secret was revealed, he was captured, had his eyes gouged out and then imprisoned. During a celebration some period later, the Philistines brought Samson out for entertainment. Somehow they lost sight that hair grows back. For Samson, that meant his strength

talents

did also. Somewhere along the way, Samson's heart returned to the task of his life. We see this in his prayer: "O Sovereign Lord, remember me. O God, please strengthen me just once more, and let me with one blow get revenge on the Philistines for my two eyes...Let me die with the Philistines!" With his last feat of strength, he killed more "when he died than while he lived" (verse 30). God didn't forsake Samson. God gave Samson what he did not deserve. God stayed close long enough for Samson to reconnect to the right power source thus bringing his service back to life. His inclusion in Hebrews 11 with other great examples of faith illustrates that it is never too late, no matter what our past, to return to service to our great God.

Feel like a failure? Feel like some diversion from the right path has ruined your chances for God to use you to advance his kingdom? As you pray today at 9am or 9pm, thank God for not throwing you out of the family. Remember your task he has given to you and thank him for allowing you to serve him and for giving your service new life.

talents

treasures

Good Morning - Day 51,

oday we move into the fourth "T," treasure. The scripture that begins this week's chapter is from Malachi. The purpose of this short book was to force the people of Israel to consider their sins and their effects on their relationship with God. In chapter three, Malachi pretty much says that unless you are giving to God you are robbing him. He gives God's instruction on giving and follows it with this promise: "Test me in this and see if I will not throw open the floodgates of heaven and pour out so much blessing that you will not have room enough for it" (v. 10).

Check out those first four words - "Test me in this." My 21st century brain interprets that as, "Come on! I dare you. Just try it. Imagine what I can do for you if you would only let me. You are only hurting yourself by robbing me. Don't you get it?" I don't know about you, but that just cracks me up. It's like God is saying, "Wake up and smell the blessings!" I believe that is why Jesus taught us to "store up for ourselves treasures in heaven" (Matt. 6:20) and why Paul told the Corinthians that they could "test the sincerity of their love" by analyzing their generosity in giving (2 Cor. 8:8).

So, have you taken the dare? Are you experiencing the blessings of giving? As you pray today at 9am or 9pm, take a moment and listen to God affirm or convict you on this subject. Whichever it is, thank him for keeping his promise or get going on testing him and seeing if it is for real.

treasures

Good Morning - Day 52,

P robably the most familiar passage in the Gospels containing Jesus' teachings is Matthew 5-7, commonly referred to as the Sermon on the Mount. It is a collection of teachings on various subjects. Close to the middle of these teachings, Jesus touches on the subject of God and money, starting in verse 19 of chapter 6. I'd like to start here and walk through some of these thoughts with you for the rest of the week. Here are the first three verses of this section:

Do not store up for yourselves treasures on earth, where moth and rust destroy, and where thieves break in and steal. 20But store up for yourselves treasures in heaven, where moth and rust do not destroy, and where thieves do not break in and steal. 21For where your treasure is, there your heart will be also.

Living in Florida we might relate more to the thought that earthly treasures are destroyed by moisture and mold. Been there? Aside from that, we can all relate to the threat of losing our treasures to thieves. Some of us have actually experienced a robbery in our homes, vehicles, or workplaces. Those are examples of intentional robberies. But other thieves are also at work right under our noses; they just don't classify themselves as such. Here's an example of what I mean. I was listening to a

treasures

church member this week tell how twice in their life they have been reminded that their attraction to collecting stuff just wasn't as important as they thought. How? The first incident was the result of an abusive marriage that ended in divorce. Divorce was the thief = Stuff gone. The second incident was living through the actions of a drug-addicted family member. Addiction was the thief = Stuff gone. Life reminded them that earthly treasures just can't compare to the eternal treasures found in living life with heaven in mind. No matter what nature the robber takes, our earthly treasures will always be susceptible to leaving us with a broken heart. God's treasures never leave us in that condition.

Looking at your treasures, is it obvious where your heart is? Is it obvious where God's treasures fit? As you pray today at 9am or 9pm, thank God for his treasures that he's made available. Commit to storing them up. Commit to letting go of the moldy treasures of earth.

treasures

Good Morning - Day 53,

Have you noticed how some drivers seem to think their driving time is the best opportunity to multitask? I admit I'm guilty of this, but seriously, some drivers just push the edge. I remember seeing this lady once who challenged my Christlike spirit when I saw her attempting to do the following: (1) turn into traffic off her street, (2) talk on the cell phone, and (3) light her cigarette. Go ahead, think through that. It's pretty much impossible. My first thought was, "Lady, when was the last time you counted how many hands you have? Are you kidding me? What are you thinking?" For all that she was trying to do she wasn't doing too badly, except for the fact that she didn't see me coming. And then some other thoughts went through my mind. Which brings me to our next verse in Matthew 6. Here's verse 24:

24No one can serve two masters. For you will hate one and love the other; you will be devoted to one and despise the other. You cannot serve both God and money. (NLT)

Here are some thoughts about this verse from an entry in the Discover God Study Bible:

> No matter how hard we try, some things require too much of our attention to allow us to do other things at the same time. When Jesus spoke of the impossibility of serving "two masters," he was addressing something similar. He was talking about

treasures

the danger of assuming you can live for two mastering passions or two over-arching life goals. It's not just hard to juggle God and money; Jesus says that it is impossible. For a follower of Jesus, this brings clarity to life--either we are receiving sustenance from him as the center of our lives or we're not. Which is it for you? Which master do you truly depend upon?[18]

As you pray today at 9am or 9pm, declare your dependence on God alone. If you feel enslaved to money, ask God to reveal to you the path to freedom. State your desire to serve him alone.

treasures

Good Morning - Day 54,

Continuing in Matthew 6, here are the next three verses:

25That is why I tell you not to worry about everyday life--whether you have enough food and drink, or enough clothes to wear. Isn't life more than food, and your body more than clothing? 26Look at the birds. They don't plant or harvest or store food in barns, for your heavenly Father feeds them. And aren't you far more valuable to him than they are? 27Can all your worries add a single moment to your life? (NLT)

Jesus acknowledges that much of our struggle to serve two masters results in or is caused by worry. He gives us some good reasons not to worry. The Life Application Bible sums them up this way:

- The same God who created life in you can be trusted with the details of your life.
- Worrying about the future hampers your efforts for today.
- Worrying is more harmful than helpful.
- God does not ignore those who depend on him.
- Worry shows a lack of faith in and understanding of God.
- There are real challenges God wants us to pursue, and worrying keeps us from them.
- Living one day at a time keeps us from being consumed with worry.[19]

So how's your worry factor? As you pray today at 9am or 9pm, disclose your worries to God - it's not like he doesn't already know them. Confess your need to have more faith in him. Ask God to give your mind a worry-free, one-day-at-a-time peace only available through him.

treasures

Good Morning - Day 55,

W ell, I said the other day that we'd look at Matthew 6 all week, but I've had another thought on my mind that I'd like to write about today and pick Matthew 6 back up tomorrow. I'd like to take you back to the opening passage of chapter 4 in our book. It came from 1 Peter 2. Here are verses 2-3:

2 Like newborn babies, crave pure spiritual milk, so that by it you may grow up in your salvation, 3 now that you have tasted that the Lord is good.

I don't know how your group discussions go, but ours are pretty good and sometime lengthy and make your mind go in different directions than you may have thought because of the discussion with others. That happened for me last night as we discussed the topic of giving/tithing. Something that I had never put into words formulated in my mind after leaving that discussion. Through a giving experience a few years ago it personally clicked for me that we should be growing in the discipline of giving throughout our entire spiritual journey. See, I grew up in a family that tithing (giving 10%) was an expectation. There was never a question. When I got my first job as a paperboy at age 12, it was expected that I would tithe off whatever I made. I have never had a period in life where I wasn't tithing. That's not a bragging comment; that's just how I was trained.

treasures

I believe the truth is that Christians never arrive at the moment where, because of what they are giving, they have no more room to grow. This was my challenge a few years ago. Until then I was pretty happy, you could probably say proud, with myself that I was giving 10% - always had and felt no reason to expect more from myself. Well, God got my attention through a fundraiser on the radio to say, "Hey, big John. Think you're pretty good, huh? Well, it's time to ante up and give a little more sacrificially. You never arrive, boy. Check your heart out and listen to what I am asking of you." Since that moment I have understood that God desires me to continuously be growing. Not just in my actions toward others by how I serve them or love them or share Christ with them or use my talents to minister to them - to be fully devoted I need to be growing in my financial giving also. The minute I think I have arrived in any spiritual discipline is the minute I need to get on my knees and admit, "I can do more. What else would you have me do?" That's my definition of "growing up in my salvation." That's the result of having "tasted the goodness of the Lord" and wanting more.

As you pray today at 9am or 9pm, be honest with God about your maturity level as it concerns the discipline of giving. If you think you've arrived, it's time to be humble before God, to grow up a little bit more. Commit to listen to God's command and submit to obey it. Let it be known that you'd like to taste more of the good stuff.

treasures

Good Morning - Day 56,

Today let's look at the next 4 verses of Matthew 6:

28And why do you worry about clothes? See how the lilies of the field grow. They do not labor or spin. 29Yet I tell you that not even Solomon in all his splendor was dressed like one of these. 30If that is how God clothes the grass of the field, which is here today and tomorrow is thrown into the fire, will he not much more clothe you, O you of little faith? 31So do not worry, saying, 'What shall we eat?' or 'What shall we drink?' or 'What shall we wear?'

In verse 29 we see a reference to Solomon. A few weeks ago we looked at him quite a bit in chapter 5. I thought of him and his writings in Ecclesiastes and wandered what he had to say about being concerned with eating, drinking, and clothes. He doesn't mentioned anything about clothes directly, but here are a few things he said about eating and drinking and taking wealth with you.

2:24-25 A man can do nothing better than to eat and drink and find satisfaction in his work. This too, I see, is from the hand of God, for without him, who can eat or find enjoyment?

5:12-15 The sleep of a laborer is sweet, whether he eats little or much, but the abundance of a rich man permits him no sleep. I have seen a grievous evil under the sun: wealth hoarded to the harm of its owner, or wealth lost through some misfortune, so that when he has a son there is nothing

treasures

left for him. Naked a man comes from his mother's womb, and as he comes, so he departs. He takes nothing from his labor that he can carry in his hand.

12:13 Now all has been heard; here is the conclusion of the matter: Fear God and keep his commandments, for this is the whole duty of man.

My assessment from reading Solomon's advice and Jesus' teachings is that when it comes to money we simply ask the wrong questions. Don't you agree? Instead of asking what is coming my way or how is it getting to me, we should be asking what can I take with me and how am I glorifying God on my daily journey. The more I rely on the hand of God the sweeter life is. The more I acknowledge anything without him is worthless the less important it becomes. The more I embrace life's eternal values the less stress I exert maintaining temporal values.

As you pray today at 9am or 9pm, ask God to help you ask the right questions. Ask him to reveal his hand to you. Commit to hold it today, to grow in performing your whole duty, and to enjoy the life he's provided for you.

treasures

Good Morning - Day 57,

Living in Florida we know all about the reactions that people have to warnings of potential dangerous weather. When we edge closer to the beginning of hurricane season, the meteorologists begin estimating how bad the season will be. Toward the end of the season, the weather channel journalists look back on the season recounting the named storms for the year. The media consistently keeps us up to date about the happenings in the tropics. It's inevitable that sometime in the season our region receives alerts issuing a hurricane watch and/or warning. Then the reactions start rolling in. They range from "I've lived here all my life and there ain't no way I'm leaving my house" to "everybody grab what's precious to you and jump in the car 'cause we're headin' to Granny's in West Virginia."

You might say that Jesus ends the Sermon on the Mount with his own alert. He makes a now familiar comparison between two reactions to his teachings. Here's the painted picture from Matthew 7:24-27:

24Therefore everyone who hears these words of mine and puts them into practice is like a wise man who built his house on the rock. 25The rain came down, the streams rose, and the winds blew and beat against that house; yet it did not fall, because it had its foundation on the rock. 26But everyone who hears these words of mine and does not put them into practice is like a foolish man who built

treasures

his house on sand. 27The rain came down, the streams rose, and the winds blew and beat against that house, and it fell with a great crash.

If you take the time to read all three chapters of the Sermon on the Mount, you realize that Jesus taught on many subjects throughout this teaching. We've just been looking at one of those subjects -God and money. So what's your reaction? Apparently, the best insurance for any money storm is having the foundation of practicing Jesus' words. I don't know about you, but my money's on investing in those words for my security and peace of mind.

As you pray today at 9am or 9pm, thank God for being the solid security source. Commit to a life built on following the teachings that promise to calm the storm, lower the flood, quiet the wind, and protect those living in the house of the wise.

treasures

Good Morning - Day 58,

ere's a story that illustrates the line, "We give to the object of our passion." (*Imagine*, 167)

His name was Fleming, and he was a poor Scottish farmer. One day while trying to make a living for his family, he heard a cry for help coming from a nearby bog. He dropped his tools and ran to the bog. There was a terrified boy mired to the waist in black muck, screaming and struggling to free himself. Farmer Fleming saved the lad from what would have been a slow and terrifying death.

The next day, a fancy carriage pulled up to the Scotsman's sparse surroundings. An eloquently dressed nobleman stepped out and introduced himself as the father of the boy.

"I want to repay you," said the nobleman. "You saved my son's life."

"No, I can't accept payment for what I did," the farmer replied, waving off the offer.

At that moment, the farmer's own son came to the door of the family hovel.

"Is that your son?" asked the nobleman.

"Yes," the farmer replied proudly.

"I'll make you a deal. Let me provide him with the level of education my son will enjoy. If the lad is

treasures

anything like his father, he'll no doubt grow to be a man we both will be proud of."
And that's exactly what the nobleman did.
Farmer Fleming's son attended the very best schools, and in time he graduated from Saint Mary's Hospital Medical School in London. He went on to become known throughout the world as the noted Sir Alexander Fleming, the discoverer of penicillin.

Years afterward, the nobleman's son was stricken with pneumonia. What saved his life this time? Penicillin.
The name of the nobleman was Lord Randolph Churchill. The nobleman's son, the one dragged from the bog, was Sir Winston Churchill. His son had been saved by the son of the farmer, the doctor who invented penicillin.[20]

These fathers gave to the object of their passions, their boys. The farmer gave his time, strength, and compassion. The nobleman gave his available resources. Their giving has now been multiplied many times over through the giving of one of their son's passions when he discovered penicillin. Who needs your gift? How available are your resources?

As you pray today at 9am or 9pm, thank God for his gifts to you. Thank him for the gift of his passion, his son. Thank him for the passions he has given you. Ask him to reveal to you how you can give to others through those passions.

treasures

Good Morning - Day 59,

O ne of the wrong ways for giving discussed in this week's chapter is giving reluctantly. Our first quiet time this week took us to Acts 4:32. That verse and the rest of that chapter give an opposite picture of reluctant giving; however if you keep reading into chapter 5 you see a very clear picture of reluctant giving through the story of Ananias and Sapphira. Read this entire passage and consider which type of giver most interests God.

32All the believers were one in heart and mind. No one claimed that any of his possessions was his own, but they shared everything they had. 33With great power the apostles continued to testify to the resurrection of the Lord Jesus, and much grace was upon them all. 34There were no needy persons among them. For from time to time those who owned lands or houses sold them, brought the money from the sales 35and put it at the apostles' feet, and it was distributed to anyone as he had need.

36Joseph, a Levite from Cyprus, whom the apostles called Barnabas (which means Son of Encouragement), 37sold a field he owned and brought the money and put it at the apostles' feet.

Acts 5

1Now a man named Ananias, together with his wife Sapphira, also sold a piece of property. 2With his wife's full knowledge he kept back part of the money for himself, but brought the rest and put it at the apostles' feet.

treasures

3Then Peter said, "Ananias, how is it that Satan has so filled your heart that you have lied to the Holy Spirit and have kept for yourself some of the money you received for the land? 4Didn't it belong to you before it was sold? And after it was sold, wasn't the money at your disposal? What made you think of doing such a thing? You have not lied to men but to God."

5When Ananias heard this, he fell down and died. And great fear seized all who heard what had happened. 6Then the young men came forward, wrapped up his body, and carried him out and buried him.

7About three hours later his wife came in, not knowing what had happened. 8Peter asked her, "Tell me, is this the price you and Ananias got for the land?"
   "Yes," she said, "that is the price."

9Peter said to her, "How could you agree to test the Spirit of the Lord? Look! The feet of the men who buried your husband are at the door, and they will carry you out also."

10At that moment she fell down at his feet and died. Then the young men came in and, finding her dead, carried her out and buried her beside her husband. 11Great fear seized the whole church and all who heard about these events.

The clear contrast can be seen in two phrases. The believers in chapter 4 were described as "no one claimed that any of his possessions was his own" while Ananias is described as "keeping back part of the money for himself." The root issue is the intent of the heart. That's why Peter

treasures

asked Ananias how he could lie to the Holy Spirit. When the Holy Spirit's directive is clear, the choice of obedience should be also. That's living the fully devoted life through our treasures.

As you pray today at 9am or 9pm, thank the Holy Spirit for his guidance. Ask him to assist you in "unclaiming" your possessions so that obedience is more natural than reluctance. After all, the smile of obedience is much more appealing than the price of reluctancy, don't you think?

treasures

Good Morning - Day 60,

Yesterday we saw an example from the early church in Acts of someone giving in the wrong way. Today let's look at two ladies who also lived in that same time who had a better mindset about giving. Their names are Tabitha and Lydia.

Here's Tabitha's story from Acts 9:

36In Joppa there was a disciple named Tabitha (which, when translated, is Dorcas), who was always doing good and helping the poor. 37About that time she became sick and died, and her body was washed and placed in an upstairs room. 38Lydda was near Joppa; so when the disciples heard that Peter was in Lydda, they sent two men to him and urged him, "Please come at once!"

39Peter went with them, and when he arrived he was taken upstairs to the room. All the widows stood around him, crying and showing him the robes and other clothing that Dorcas had made while she was still with them.

40Peter sent them all out of the room; then he got down on his knees and prayed. Turning toward the dead woman, he said, "Tabitha, get up." She opened her eyes, and seeing Peter she sat up. 41He took her by the hand and helped her to her feet. Then he called the believers and the widows and presented her to them alive. 42This became known all over Joppa, and many people believed in the Lord.

treasures

I have a hunch that all these mourners were so moved by her passing because of her giving nature. Did you notice how the widows remembered Tabitha in verse 39? Tabitha evidently believed that her time, talents, and treasures were not hers but God's.

Here's Lydia's story from Acts 16:

11From Troas we put out to sea and sailed straight for Samothrace, and the next day on to Neapolis. 12From there we traveled to Philippi, a Roman colony and the leading city of that district of Macedonia. And we stayed there several days.

13On the Sabbath we went outside the city gate to the river, where we expected to find a place of prayer. We sat down and began to speak to the women who had gathered there. 14One of those listening was a woman named Lydia, a dealer in purple cloth from the city of Thyatira, who was a worshiper of God. The Lord opened her heart to respond to Paul's message. 15When she and the members of her household were baptized, she invited us to her home. "If you consider me a believer in the Lord," she said, "come and stay at my house." And she persuaded us.

Lydia was a new believer and had just met Paul and his companions. Already she knew that her house was not hers alone. Her new faith led her to immediate obedience.

These ladies through simple gestures illustrate to us lives that knew the source of their possessions. As you pray today at 9am or 9pm, ask God to reveal to you who in your life may need a simple gesture through your giving. Also ask him to continue to grow your heart to be the heart of a giver.

treasures

Good Morning - Day 61,

T oday I'd like to look at another lady, this time from 1 Kings, who also gives us an excellent example of giving in the right way. I don't know if you'd classify her giving as cheerful, but I can assure you it was sacrificial.

We don't know her name; we only know her as the widow at Zarephath. Apparently she at one time was a woman of means because her house contained an upper room. But with the loss of her husband and the recent famine, she was now extremely poor. We meet her in chapter 17 gathering sticks by the gate of her village. God's prophet Elijah has just come through the gates and has picked her out to ask for a drink of water and a bite of bread. Let's pick the story up in verse 12:

"But she said, 'I swear by the Lord your God that I don't have a single piece of bread in the house. And I have only a handful of flour left in the jar and a little cooking oil in the bottom of the jug. I was just gathering a few sticks to cook this last meal, and then my son and I will die.'
But Elijah said to her, 'Don't be afraid! Go ahead and do just what you've said, but make a little bread for me first. Then use what's left to prepare a meal for yourself and your son. For this is what the Lord, the God of Israel, says: There will always be flour and olive oil left in your containers until the time when the Lord sends rain and the crops grow again!' So she did as Elijah said, and she and Elijah and her son continued to eat for many days. There was always enough flour and olive oil left in the containers, just as the Lord had promised through Elijah." (NLT)

I can't say I've been where this lady was, but I'll try to walk a mile in her shoes for a moment. A stranger approaches her and asks for a drink and something to eat. Ok, no big deal, right? Oh wait - there's a famine going on. Can you imagine how many

treasures

people may have been wandering the streets looking for the same thing? For all we know she's been asked this same question several times over the last week and feels like she should be asking the same thing. Meanwhile this stranger throws in this bit about if she'd just make his bread first then his God will somehow pull off some magic trick and keep her stocked until the famine is over. If I were in her shoes I'd have been very tempted to say, "I was thinking about it until you brought up that crazy idea that you somehow are connected to the God of Israel."

But, since I don't know Ms. Widow, maybe that's all she needed to know. Maybe the people of Zarephath had heard of the God of Israel and just how throughout history he had done some incredible things for them, provided what was definitely the impossible. Maybe for the first time in months she was given a glimmer of hope. But why did it have to include a test of faith, a test of sacrifice? Apparently she decided it was worth the risk, worth the sacrifice. Death was coming anyway so why not give it a shot. And look at what the God of Israel did. He did for her what she'd heard he'd done for his people. He kept his promise. The momentary sacrifice was all she needed to do to receive the abundance of God's kept promise.

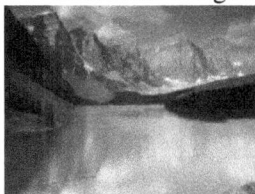

Do you feel like you're in a famine? Are you gathering the sticks? Has it caused you to question the promises of your God? If so, as you pray today at 9am or 9pm, put it all out there. After you've shown him the empty canister, then sit still and let him bring to mind how he has provided for you and others throughout history. Let him remind you that he is still God. Let the God of Israel speak to you and assure you the famine will end, the rain is coming, the crops will grow again, and until then he's got you covered.

treasures

Good Morning - Day 62,

Two of our quiet times for this last week include passages from Matthew and Luke which record the story of the rich man who asked Jesus, "Good Teacher, what should I do to inherit eternal life?" In an earlier email we looked at his decision to not follow Jesus' directive to sell all his possessions and give the money to the poor. Following that decision the young man left, and Jesus, seeing a teachable moment, seized it to teach about the challenge the rich have when facing the decision of truly following God in all aspects of their lives. Luke records the end of this teaching with this statement by Jesus:

"...I assure you that everyone who has given up house or wife or brothers or parents or children, for the sake of the kingdom of God, will be repaid many times over in this life, and will have eternal life in the world to come." (18:29-30, NLT)

Now we're getting deep. Do you know any missionaries? If not, have you ever considered the sacrifice they make to give up their lives on Main Street, leaving their family, friends, and church body to go somewhere they've never been purely to advance the kingdom of God? Or even the sacrifice that many ministers in general make along these same lines? Does that seem like something you may say, "Well, thank God, he hasn't asked me to do that"?

treasures

Hold that thought. Hasn't he? The fully devoted life means the kingdom of God - pursuing his work in my life and others' - has first priority. Nothing or no one comes before him. Does that mean everyone has to sell their house in order to truly be a devoted follower of Christ? Well, in some cases, God probably is saying that. But the true issue here is your heart. Are you willing to give

up whatever God says in order for his kingdom to be more alive in you and to be more apparent and available for others? You might reword that question, just how do you define being rich anyway?

As you pray today at 9am or 9pm, ask God to reveal to you your role in advancing his kingdom. If he tells you, "You're doing it. Keep it up," thank him for the encouragement. If he reveals some changes need to happen, ask him for the strength and wisdom to follow through for the sake of the kingdom.

treasures

Good Morning - Day 63,

ere's a quote from this week's chapter: "Grace is giving people what they don't deserve... The grace we receive from God, a love that we don't deserve, causes us to be more compassionate toward people who also need to receive God's love. The love we receive provides the energy and motivation to invest." (*Imagine*, 170)

Reading this reminded me of a Michael W. Smith song he released in 1992 on his *Change Your World* album. Below are the lyrics to that song, "Give it Away."

She asked him for forever
And a promise that would last
He said, "Babe, you know I love you
But I can't commit to that";
She said "Love isn't love
'Til you give it away";
A father lived in silence
Saw his son become a man
There was a distance felt between them
'Cause he could not understand
That love isn't love
'Til you give it away
You gotta give it away

treasures

Chorus:
As we live
Moving side by side
May we learn to give
Learn to sacrifice

We can entertain compassion
For a world in need of care
But the road of good intentions
Doesn't lead to anywhere
'Cause love isn't love
'Til you give it away
You gotta give it away

Chorus

Bridge:
Love is like a river
Flowing down from the giver of life
We drink from the water
And our thirst is no longer denied
You gotta give it away

Chorus

There was a man who walked on water
He came to set the people free
He was the ultimate example
Of what love can truly be
'Cause his love was his life
And he gave it away
You gotta give it away

Chorus[21]

treasures

The end of these lyrics reference Jesus' giving it away. Remember his grace to the dying thief beside him? And how about his gracious request to his father, "Forgive them, for they don't know what they are doing?" (Luke 23:34, NLT) He clearly illustrated the love we can have which will provide us the energy and motivation to invest - to give it away.

As you pray today at 9am or 9pm, thank Jesus for his grace, his sacrifice, his love, his investing, his giving it away. Ask the Holy Spirit to help you grow in giving it away.

treasures

celebration

Good Morning - Day 64,

We are calling this final Imagine weekend Celebration Weekend to note the culmination of our Imagine journey. I thought in today's note we'd look at a Psalm to help us celebrate our thanks to our God. This is Psalm 100 (NLT):

Shout with joy to the Lord, all the earth!
Worship the Lord with gladness. Come before him, singing with joy.
Acknowledge that the Lord is God!
He made us, and we are his.
We are his people, the sheep of his pasture.
Enter his gates with thanksgiving; go into his courts with praise.
Give thanks to him and praise his name.
For the Lord is good.
His unfailing love continues forever, and his faithfulness continues to each generation.

As you pray today at 9am or 9pm, I encourage you to do something a little out of the ordinary. Read those 9 lines from Psalm 100 out loud. If possible, get your whole household around and read it together. Let God know that you celebrate who he is, what he has done, and what his unfailing love and faithfulness has yet to do.

celebration

Good morning - Day 65,

You know the saying that love is a two-way street, right? Well, let's acknowledge that with God.

Yesterday we celebrated him by reading Psalm 100. Are you aware that Scripture says he wants to celebrate us? Do you remember reading the parable of the three servants in Matthew 25 this week in our first quiet time? Check out the last phrase in verses 21 and 23. The master said to the servants who had served him well, "Let's celebrate together!" (NLT) Now read this verse from Zephaniah 3:17: "For the Lord your God is living among you. He is a mighty savior. He will take delight in you with gladness. With his love, he will calm all your fears. He will rejoice over you with joyful songs." (NLT) I envision him standing off to the side like a father at his daughter's wedding just waiting to get his chance to dance with her in a celebration of love. Reminds me of the following lyrics of the praise song, "Amazed":

You dance over me
While I am unaware
You sing all around
But I never hear the sound

Lord I'm amazed by You
Lord I'm amazed by You

celebration

Lord I'm amazed by You
How You love me
How wide
How deep
How great
Is Your love for me[22]

As you pray today at 9am or 9pm, I encourage you to do another unusual thing. Stand in the middle of the room right where you are. For your prayer, just ask God to shower you with messages of his love. If you feel like dancing, it's okay. If you feel like falling on your knees, it's okay. If you feel like lifting your hands, it's okay. If you feel like just bowing your head and crying your eyes out, it's okay. Just soak it in. Let the two-way communication flow.

celebration

End Notes

Day 4
[1]Anna B. Warner and William B. Bradbury, "Jesus loves me," *Living Hymns* (Montrose, PA: Encore Publications, 1972), 708.

[2]Fanny J. Crosby and Joseph F. Knapp, "Blessed Assurance," *Living Hymns* (Montrose, PA: Encore Publications, 1972), 51.

Day 6
[3]John Hagee, *The Seven Secrets: Unlocking Genuine Greatness* (Lake Mary, FL: Charisma House, 2004), 153-154.

Day 7
[4]*Discover God Study Bible*, New Living Translation (Carol Stream, IL: Tyndale House Publishers, 2007), 2181.

Day 12
[5]Anne Graham Lotz, *God's Story: Finding Meaning for Your Life* (Dallas, TX: Word, 1997), 3.

Day 13
[6]"Were You There?" Traditional Spiritual, *The Celebration Hymnal: Songs and Hymns for Worship* (Word Music/Integrity Music, 1997), 315.

Day 16
[7]Garry Poole, "Rita Prayed," *Willow*, Fall 2007, 46.

Day 21
[8]"Amish Forgiveness," PaDutch.com, http://www.800padutch.com/amishforgiveness.shtml

Day 28
[9]Margaret Becker/Tedd T./Brent Milligan/Dave Lichens, "Horses," *Falling Forward* (Brentwood, TN: Sparrow Records, 1998).

Day 31
[10]Bruce Barcott, "Life and Limb," *Runner's World*, October 2008, http://www.runnersworld.com/article/0,7120,s6-243-297--12959-0,00.html

Day 32
[11]Richard Niell Donovan, "Hymn Story: Take Time to be Holy," lectionary.org, Copyright © 2006. http://www.lectionary.org/HymnStories/Take%20Time%20to%20Be%20Holy.htm

Day 37
[12]Bill Whitaker, "From Sandbox to Carnegie Hall," cbsnews.com, October 9, 2008, http://www.cbsnews.com/stories/2008/10/09/eveningnews/main4512497.shtml

Day 39
[13]"The Human Need for Touch and Growth in Consumer Electronics," January 16, 2008, http://marketingbeyond.typepad.com/marketingbeyond/2008/01/the-human-need.html

[14]Max Lucado, *Just Like Jesus* (Nashville, TN: Word, 1998), 34-36.

Day 40
[15]Civilla D. Martin and Charles H. Gabriel, "His Eye is on the Sparrow," cyberhymnal.org, September 21, 2008, http://www.cyberhymnal.org/htm/h/i/hiseyeis.htm

Day 44
[16]Jimmy Roberts, "Cousins' Impact on Atlanta," nbcsports.com, September 27, 2008, http://nbcsports.msnbc.com/id/22825103/vp/2615357#26915357 Tom Cousins, nbc

Day 45
[17]"'How do I say no' to the limbless," CNN.com, August 22, 2008, http://www.cnn.com/2008/LIVING/wayoflife/08/22/heroes.puckett/index.html

Day 53
[18]*Discover God Study Bible*, New Living Translation (Carol Stream, IL: Tyndale House Publishers, 2007), 1754.

Day 54
[19]*Life Application Study Bible*, New International Version (Wheaton, IL: Tyndale House Publishers; Grand Rapids, MI: Zondervan, 1991), 1659.

Day 58
[20]John Hagee, *The Seven Secrets: Unlocking Genuine Greatness* (Lake Mary, FL: Charisma House, 2004), 213-214.

Day 63
[21]Michael W. Smith, "Give It Away," *Change Your World* (Franklin, TN: Reunion Records, 1992).

Day 65
[22]Jared Anderson, "Amazed," *Vertical Worship Songs* (Integrity Music, 2004).